Speed & Agility
REVOLUTION

Movement Training for Athletic Success

Jim Kielbaso

CREW PRESS

Kielbaso, Jim
    Speed & Agility Revolution / Jim Kielbaso

ISBN # 0-9762944-0-0

Library of Congress Control Number: 2004099358

Copyright © 2005 Crew Press. All rights reserved. Printed in the United States.

No part of this book may be reproduced, stored in a retrieval system, or transmitted, in any form or by any means, electronic, mechanical, photocopying, or otherwise, without the prior permission of Crew Press.

Throughout this book, the masculine shall be deemed the feminine and vice versa.

Cover Design: Dan Savich
Editor: Jim Person

Crew Press
1298 Ann Arbor Trail
Plymouth, MI 48170
www.crewpress.com

Table of Contents

Professional Acknowledgements

John Frappier
Ken Mannie
Tim Wakeham
Bob Vezeau
Matt Brzycki
Anne Yoches
Glenn Terry
Walt Reynolds
Mike Gittleson
Tim Daly
Ian Lauer
Mickey Marotti
Daren DeCavitte
Bob Scheuer
Jason Cole
Mike Vorkapich
Tony Rolinski
Nick Wilson
Jack Vivian
Greg Baker

Introduction

Every athlete wants to get faster, and every coach wants his/her athletes to stop and start quicker, cut harder, and move more efficiently. I see athletes of all ages, in all different sports, all over the world performing drills they think will improve their athleticism. Coaches put out cones, ladders, hurdles, and hoops in all sorts of patterns and designs hoping they will find the magic drill that will transform their athletes into the next Michael Jordan, Barry Sanders, Andre Agassi, Mia Hamm or Renaldo.

The drills are usually appropriate, but the biggest problem I see is that they simply are not being used in the most beneficial way possible. A lot of coaches come up with interesting and creative patterns for agility drills, and I commend them for their innovation. Unfortunately, most coaches believe that the *drills* are the key to performance enhancement. They borrow drills from college and professional coaches, or see different exercises in books and magazines, and assume that if elite athletes are performing these drills, they must be good for their athletes.

The truth is, just about any agility drill can be used to effectively enhance the movement patterns of an athlete, but it's not the *drill* that is important – it is the *coaching and instruction* that can make a real impact on an athlete. It is absolutely imperative for the coach who is implementing the drill to understand proper movement mechanics, analyze the movement patterns of his/her athletes, and be able to provide effective instruction and corrective feedback. Without these skills, the coach is not really helping the athletes by simply having them run through drill after drill. This book contains the information necessary to break down athletic movement patterns and successfully program the human body to move in the most efficient way possible.

While this book includes many speed and agility drills, I hope you don't skip right to that section and start using them in your workouts. The most important parts of this book are the technique instruction and coaching cues that have the potential to dramatically improve the way an athlete moves. If the drills are used without proper technique, you will not make nearly as much long-term progress as if you slow down, and take the time to learn more efficient movement patterns.

A basketball coach would never have a player work on his jump shot for an hour without correcting technique flaws. What kind of coach would allow a player to continue to shoot with his elbow sticking out and his wrist stiff under the ball? Would the same coach work on team defense strategies if his players can't even get into a solid defensive stance?

Or, would you ever see a tennis coach have a player practice her serve without correcting poor serving mechanics? Would a pitching or hitting coach in baseball or softball allow his athletes to perform drills for hours without correcting mechanical errors?

The answer to all of these questions is NO! Good coaches know that drills are only tools which are used to practice technique. And most athletes have no interest in wasting time and energy on drills that are not going to make them better athletes. No drill will magically make an athlete better if proper technique is not emphasized. Why is it, then, that so many coaches and athletes simply line up cones and ladders for agility work, but never correct faulty mechanics? This would be like having a golf pro tell you to hit balls for an hour, but he/she never provides you with any feedback or instruction. Why bother practicing if you're doing it wrong? This is happening because many coaches simply lack an understanding of proper movement mechanics and how to get athletes to perform them correctly.

I have had the good fortune of working with, and learning from, some great coaches and athletes. One thing I have learned from them is that they are all willing to take a step backward to work on technique before they try to move forward. Laying a solid foundation has a much greater long-term impact than any quick fix. Would you build a million dollar home on a foundation of sand? I wouldn't.

Good coaches understand that slowing down to learn proper mechanics will ultimately allow an athlete to excel. Initially, the new techniques may feel awkward to the athlete, but coaches know that the new movement patterns will feel more natural with practice. Ultimately, this will yield much better results than allowing athletes to run through drills utilizing poor technique.

A brief review of the motor learning literature will teach us a valuable lesson about inadequate coaching. All of the available literature in this area tells us that allowing athletes to perform speed and agility drills with poor technique will only help to reinforce those faulty movement patterns. It seems obvious when you think about other sport skills, such as a golf swing, but the problem continues in the area of speed and agility work.

It is exciting for me to get this information into the hands of coaches and practitioners who work with our young athletes every day. I truly believe that getting coaches to understand and apply the principles outlined in this book could revolutionize the way athletes learn how to move.

This book is just the beginning. As other professionals begin to look at speed and agility from this perspective, our understanding of movement patterns will continue to improve and our athletes will ultimately benefit from new thinking. In the future, researchers will create a much greater understanding of movement mechanics, and the concepts presented in this book will certainly be improved.

The References section of this book provides a list of articles and studies that can be reviewed if a more in-depth understanding of these concepts is desired. This book has taken all of the relevant scientific information, blended it with the practical experience of training thousands of athletes, and created a more complete system of speed and agility training. Until now, this information simply was not available to most coaches.

At first, it may seem unnatural or awkward to change the movement patterns of an athlete. Start the process slowly, and apply only what you feel comfortable dealing with. You don't have to use everything in this book all at once. The point is to start looking at athletes in a new way that emphasizes quality movement.

You are the key to making this happen. As you will see throughout this book, speed and agility drills are only as valuable as the coach implementing them. You already know that you have the opportunity to make a significant impact on the lives of many athletes, and your role has just expanded. You now have the knowledge to dramatically improve the way a person moves. This is an exciting opportunity, and I hope you join me in this speed and agility revolution.

Chapter 1

Foundations of Speed & Agility

Compared to other topics involved in sport performance there is a relatively small amount of scientific information available on speed and agility. There have been a decent number of studies published about different aspects of speed, but the area of agility is largely unexplored. Taking this a step further, there is a huge lack of scientific information available that explains how to develop these important physical traits. Most of the literature on the topic of speed and agility focuses on training methods rather than the scientific basis of why those methods actually work.

To fully understand the science behind these training methods would require a great deal of time studying anatomy, physiology, biomechanics, and motor learning. Instead, most of the science involved in these methods boils down to one concept: adaptation.

The two main components that require adaptation in order to improve speed and agility performance are the nervous system and the contractile fibers of the musculature. Most training methods are designed to improve the function of one, or both, of these components. The basic purpose of strength training is to force the involved musculature to adapt to the training by increasing the size or strength of the tissue; the muscles get stronger due to the training. Adding strength to the available musculature allows the body to execute movements with increased force. Increasing the potential muscular force will create greater velocity and more powerful movement in any direction.

The nervous system works in a similar way with speed and agility training. When an athlete wants to perform a specific movement, the nervous system responds by sending impulses to the appropriate muscles. The nervous system tells the muscles how fast, how hard, and in which sequence to contract to create the movement pattern. Once the basic pattern is established, the nervous system will adapt to additional practice by adjusting the number of fibers needed, sequence in which they need to fire, etc. So, the more you practice a movement, the better you get. But practice doesn't always make perfect. *Perfect practice* is necessary if you're looking for meaningful results.

It is of vital importance to make sure that all movement training is done with impeccable technique so the nervous system has the opportunity to create the most effective neural pathways possible. The motor learning literature suggests that several weeks of purposeful training can create what is known as a motor engram. This is a neural pathway that is so strong that it no longer requires cognitive effort to properly execute. Some people call this muscle memory (even though this is not really an accurate name) because your body learns to perform the movement without thought.

Many coaches claim that you cannot coach speed, but this is an untrue statement. Of course, there is a genetic limit to the amount of improvement that any individual can make, but great improvements can certainly be made in most individuals. As a person approaches his/her genetic potential, improvements will become smaller and more difficult to elicit, but hard work and proper training will certainly benefit any athlete.

Empirical evidence suggests that initiating training at a young age and focusing on challenging the nervous system can raise the potential abilities of an athlete. This training would focus on body awareness, control and the proper execution of specific movement patterns such as sprinting and directional change mechanics.

It also seems that there is more room for improvement in agility than in straight-ahead speed. This is certainly not conclusive scientific evidence, but many athletes seem to have the potential to improve agility to a greater extent than sprint speed. Fortunately, improving agility seems to be a more important factor in many competitive situations than improving top-end speed.

More research needs to be done in this area to both validate training methods and help coaches create optimal programs. Until then, the application of the basic science behind speed and agility training seems pretty clear. We need to practice specific movement patterns in order to enhance function, and it is important to incorporate strength training in an effort to increase the potential force that can be created in any movement.

When analyzing the science behind training, it is also important to understand the three basic components of sports performance:

1. Physical Ability: Speed, agility, conditioning, strength, power, flexibility, etc.
2. Technical Skills: Catching, throwing, shooting, passing, dribbling, trapping, play execution, etc.
3. Tactical Understanding: Game awareness, reading plays, recognizing opponents' tendencies, decision making, etc.

Technical and tactical skills are crucial for success in athletics, but there are other books that concentrate on specific technical and tactical aspects of each sport. Each of these components will be addressed briefly, but *the focus of this book is on improving the physical abilities involved in many sports.*

The ability to stop, start, and change directions is commonly referred to as agility. It is important to note that agility is not as cut and dry as sprint mechanics because the multi-directional movements seen in sports are typically performed in reaction to an external stimulus (i.e. an opponent). It must be understood, then, that agility movements can be broken into two categories:

    a.   Closed Loop Skills
    b.   Open Loop Skills

Closed Skills

Closed-loop movements are performed with a pre-determined starting point and finish. They do not require the Central Nervous System (CNS) to process feedback from external stimuli in order to properly perform the movement; they do not require the athlete to react to an opponent or environmental change. Examples of closed skills include:

    Golf swing
    Basketball free throw
    All gymnastics events
    Track & field events
    Punting or kicking a football
    Weightlifting events
    Power lifting events

> Diving
> Figure skating
> Tennis serve

Essentially, these skills can be practiced over and over until the nervous system has "memorized" the patterns into a motor engram. There will always be external pressures such as a noisy crowd or competing against a rival, but these pressures do not affect the actual skill being performed. The athlete does not need to adjust his/her gymnastics floor routine to another competitor; the flooring is always the same (to a certain degree), the music and skills are pre-determined and the entire routine can be practiced exactly as it will be performed in competition. The mechanics of a basketball free throw do not need to change because the basket is moving; the hoop is always the same height and the foul line is always the same distance from the hoop. The high jumper does not need to react to or evade a defender before take off; the obstacle is stationary and the athlete can pace-off the distance from the line in which he/she begins the approach.

In closed-skill events, the athlete is essentially competing with him/herself to perform a sports skill in competition. The skill can be started and finished whenever the athlete chooses (to a certain degree; there are generally time limits on these events) without any external interference. Once the movement is initiated, the body can react to internal feedback. For example, in the middle of a dive, a diver may realize he needs to rotate faster to properly complete the required number of rotations before he hits the water; he can then adjust his body accordingly to increase rotational speed. But, it is not necessary to react to external factors such as moving targets in the water or opponents crossing his path in mid-flight.

It almost seems humorous to think of external factors being involved in traditionally closed-skill performances. Closed-skill sports are already so incredibly technical that they are difficult enough without having to deal with external feedback. Just think how difficult it would be to perform a balance beam routine with opponents throwing balls at the gymnast. Or imagine how interesting it would be if the 4 x 100 relay race were a full contact event. (Hmmm, perhaps we're on to something here.)

Open Skills

Open-loop skills require the athlete to process information from external stimuli and react accordingly. The athlete must take external information, such as the positioning of opponents, process it through the CNS, then produce movement patterns that appropriately deal with this information. Examples of open skills include:

> A tennis player moving across the court to retrieve an opponent's shot
> A football running back evading an oncoming defender
> A soccer goalie diving for a shot
> A basketball player adjusting her jump shot in the air to avoid a block
> A rugby player tackling a moving offensive player
> A wrestler executing a takedown against an opponent trying to avoid the move
> A boxer blocking a punch, then countering with his own combination
> A football defensive back reading a play and intercepting the pass
> A baseball batter adjusting his swing to a change-up pitch

You can see that all of these skills require practice, but all of these athletes must process external information in order to execute the appropriate movements. There is no pre-determined beginning or end of each movement, as this is determined in response to external cues.

Interestingly, if an athlete takes too long to "think about" the reaction to the external stimuli, he/she will generally appear very slow on the field or court. This is a where reaction time and response time need to be addressed.

Reaction Time vs. Response Time

Reaction time is the amount of time it takes an athlete to process the external stimuli and *initiate* a physical response. Response time, on the other hand, is the amount of time it takes to process the external stimuli, decide on the appropriate response, and actually *complete* the physical response. Reaction time is dependent on cognitive ability and neural efficiency, while response time is heavily dependent on those aspects, as well as physical ability. Response time is basically reaction time plus the physical response. This can be very confusing, but in order to maximize individual potential and play a game as effectively as possible, both of these aspects must be taken into consideration.

Practicing speed and agility drills can improve response time, but will not necessarily improve reaction time. Reaction time can be improved through external recognition drills and practicing pre-determined responses to external cues. This sounds very complex, and it can be, but let's try to simplify all of this.

First of all, it is important to note that most agility drills are practiced in closed environments. Cones are set up in varying patterns, ladder drills are performed with a stationary apparatus, shuttles are timed to impress coaches, etc. In all of these situations, the athlete does not need to react to an oppositional stimuli or opponent. This is a completely acceptable part of agility practice as long as you recognize that these drills should be used as a way to teach the proper mechanics involved in open-skill situations, not as complete agility training.

Far too often, athletes perform agility drills just to get through the drill. Then they perform improper technique during a game and wonder why the drills are not improving their performance. Athletes need to understand that practicing agility drills in closed environments is done to teach the nervous system how to properly execute the skills during competition. The proper execution of these basic movement patterns needs to be practiced over and over until they can be properly performed without thought during a competition. If an athlete is thinking about his foot placement (internal feedback) during a directional change in the middle of a football game, there is a good chance that the external stimulus is not receiving the attention it deserves. To simplify this, if a running back is worried about sprinting mechanics as he comes through a hole, he's probably not going to notice the linebacker who is about to put him on his back.

Agility mechanics must be properly practiced in a repetitive fashion the same way sprinting mechanics are practiced over and over again. Unfortunately, many coaches don't pay attention to the biomechanics involved in directional changes, and agility drills are used as conditioning drills. Make no mistake, many agility drills can be used to efficiently condition athletes, but learning and executing proper technique during these drills is of paramount importance.

Once the neural pathways involved in a specific movement are solidified through closed skill practice, they may be utilized in an open loop environment such as competition. If the neural pathways are not strong, however, that skill will probably not be performed correctly in the heat of a competition.

When an athlete can properly execute directional changes, it can greatly decrease response time because more efficient movement patterns are being utilized. This will allow the athlete to get into position faster with a decreased likelihood of injury.

On the other hand, in order to improve reaction time, a great deal of time and effort must be spent understanding the intricacies of the game being played, i.e. tactical skills. Athletes with limited physical abilities can excel if they can anticipate and put themselves in proper position to make a play. Many athletes excel in physical tests such as the 40-yard dash or Pro Agility Shuttle, yet appear quite slow on the field. Other athletes are average at those tests, but look amazing on the field. These athletes are able to read the play so well that they initiate appropriate movements well before their opponents. Their reaction time is quicker because of superior cognitive processing abilities.

Coaches can help improve reaction time by teaching athletes what to look for in specific situations. Then, to really make improvements, coaches should give these athletes a limited number of responses to each external cue. For example, soccer defensemen should be taught to recognize when an opponent is making a run toward the goal. Or, a quarterback should be taught how to read a defense at the line so he can anticipate how the called play is going to work after the snap. When this can be picked up, the athlete should be given one or two responses to the external cue. They should be instructed exactly how to defend the attack, or which options to look for, and should be given the opportunity to practice the recognition and reaction pattern over and over again until it can be performed with limited cognitive processing. It should be more of an instinct than a conscious decision.

When athletes can easily recognize external cues, they may have the feeling of everything happening in slow motion. Without the ability to recognize external cues, athletes will always be late in their response and will have to rely on superior physical ability to make plays.

Finally, superior athletic performance will never be achieved without excellent technical skills. It doesn't matter how fast a receiver can run if he can't catch a ball. A soccer player must be able to trap, pass and dribble the ball efficiently if success is expected. Basketball players must be able to dribble and shoot if they expect to make an impact on the game. In my opinion, more time must be spent on technical skills than any other area. This is especially true for younger athletes.

If you have a basketball team with five great athletes, but they can't dribble or shoot, you're success is going to be limited. On the other hand, if you have five average athletes who can dribble like former Harlem Globetrotter Curly Neal, and shoot like Larry Bird, they're going to be pretty hard to stop. Obviously, having athletes with great physical, technical and tactical skills is the optimal situation, but technical skills must be the foundation.

An amazingly large number of basketball and soccer players claim that they need "first step explosiveness," but upon closer examination, it is their fundamental ball handling skills that need work. Take a lighting-quick basketball player like Allen Iverson and put a soccer ball at his feet, and see how explosive his first step looks. Conversely, put a basketball in Renaldo's hands, and watch one of the world's most explosive athletes move like Mrs. Butterworth. If you don't have great technical skills, improving physical abilities will be of limited value.

So, if you want to improve the speed, agility and quickness of your athletes (or yourself), it is essential that you practice from both the neck up and the neck down. All professional athletes have exceptional physical and technical abilities, yet they still watch game films and practice situational drills for hours at a time in an effort to improve their cognitive ability to recognize external tactical cues and decrease reaction time.

Sound coaching, and situational practice is extremely important, but this needs to be addressed differently for each sport and position. Including detailed information for each and every sport and position is way beyond the scope of this book. Response time, on the other hand, is what this book and the drills involved will help you improve.

Notes

Chapter 2

Warm-Up & Flexibility

Warm-Up

Before engaging in any speed or agility training, a thorough warm-up should be completed to prepare the body for what is ahead. A warm-up will last 5-8 minutes, will raise the body's core temperature, and will involve movement of all the joints and muscles that will be used in training. The following warm-up routine has been used by thousands of athletes and is a straightforward approach to preparing the body for any kind of movement training. It involves movement in several directions, lasts 5-8 minutes, includes light stretching, and will get most athletes to break a light sweat. This routine can easily be modified to meet the specific needs of different athletes.

Find an area 15-20 yards long. Perform one lap (down & back) of each of the following movements:
1. Jog
2. Backpedal
3. High-Knee Walk
4. High-Knee Run
5. Butt Kicks
6. Skips
7. Power Skips (skipping as high as possible)
8. Step-Slide Walks
9. Shuffle
10. Carioca
11. 10 Squat Jumps (in place)

When these 11 drills are completed, do the following stretches holding each one (where applicable) for only 5-10 seconds.
1. Arm Circles – 5 times forward, 5 times backward (large circles)
2. Trunk Twists – 10 twists
3. Standing Calf Stretch
4. Hip Flexor Stretch
5. Standing Hamstring Stretch
6. Standing Groin Stretch
7. Standing Quad Stretch
8. Ankle Rotations
9. Low Back Rotations – 2 each way

The following pages contain pictures of some of the warm-up drills and stretches mentioned above.

High-Knee Walk

High-Knee Run

Trunk Twist 1

Step Slide Walk 1

Step Slide Walk 2

Trunk Twist 2

Standing Calf Stretch

Hip Flexor Stretch

Standing Hamstring Stretch

Standing Groin Stretch

Standing Quad Stretch

Ankle Rotations

Low Back Rotation 1

2

3

4

5

Flexibility

There are more complete books available on flexibility which are highly recommended if you are looking for advanced information on this topic. The flexibility section of this book is intended to give the reader some basic information for starting a program. There are hundreds of different stretches and routines, but going into great depth on this topic is beyond the intended scope of this book. This book shows basic stretches that are appropriate for many athletes, but there are a plethora of specialized stretches that are used for specific problems.

While flexibility is certainly an integral part of athleticism, perhaps too much has been made of its importance to speed and agility. Many coaches and trainers believe that increasing flexibility as much as possible will allow the muscles to move more freely through their range of motion, thus allowing for faster movement speeds. The theory is that very loose muscles have less resistance to movement at great speeds, and that increased range of motion helps safeguard against injuries. While this may be partially true, it is not completely accurate, and there is no scientific evidence to support this theory.

It is important to have enough flexibility to perform the sport skills required of the athlete without restriction. "Enough" flexibility is that which allows a muscle to move through its entire range of motion freely and efficiently. A joint can only move through its complete range of motion when all of the muscles acting upon it have sufficient flexibility. If any areas are tight or restrictive, the muscles and joints around the area are more susceptible to injury and will not perform optimally. When this is the case, a flexibility program is critical.

If, however, the athlete has enough flexibility to perform all sporting movements without restriction, the importance of an intense flexibility program drops significantly. This is not to say that the athlete should not stretch at all, but increasing flexibility well beyond this point may be unnecessary, and does not need to be a major focus of training.

The key to making this determination is the proper assessment of flexibility. Without specialized training, a thorough assessment is rather difficult for most coaches, and it is recommended that a physical therapist (or similarly trained professional) be consulted if there is a concern. From this consultation, the coach should easily be able to help implement the suggestions made by the professional.

But, increasing flexibility beyond what is necessary will not necessarily improve performance. In fact, too much flexibility may be somewhat dangerous. There is a difference between active flexibility and passive flexibility that needs to be understood.

Active flexibility is the amount of movement that can be performed without any external assistance. For example, from a standing position, see how high you can lift your leg straight out in front of you. This is active flexibility. You are *actively* able to place your body in this position using your own strength. Now, have someone grab your foot and raise your leg as high as possible. You will notice that your leg will go higher with some external assistance. Your muscles do not have to actively place your leg in this position, so this is considered passive flexibility.

The greater the difference between your active and passive flexibility, the greater the amount of uncontrollable movement around a joint. This may be somewhat dangerous because you cannot control all of the movement available to you. There will always be a difference between the active and passive range of motion, but athletes should attempt to limit this by strengthening the muscles while increasing flexibility.

Increasing your flexibility beyond what is necessary has not been shown to improve performance. Many athletes believe that amazing amounts of flexibility will help them run faster, but this is not supported by any scientific study. Certainly, a lack of flexibility will have a negative impact on speed because stride length and running mechanics will be affected, but there is no evidence that suggests being able to pull your foot behind your head will make you run faster. If you cannot adequately perform the skills required of your sport, there is certainly a need to improve your flexibility. But, if you have no problem performing all of the movements required of your sport, it is unnecessary to spend a great deal of time improving flexibility.

Stretching is an important component of a well-rounded training program, but the amount of time and energy spent on this area will vary greatly depending upon the needs of each athlete. A gymnast or martial artist will spend much more time developing flexibility than a basketball player because those sports call for greater flexibility. It is somewhat important for a first-baseman to be able to stretch into the splits, so time must be spent on this. A third-baseman on the other hand, does not need to do the splits, so less of an emphasis will be placed on this.

Developing Flexibility

Developing flexibility is similar to developing strength. Strength is developed when the intensity of the stimulus (workout) is great enough to force an adaptation in the musculature. A demanding training program will force the muscles to increase the size of the contractile fibers so that more weight can be lifted. This happens over a long period of time, requires a great deal of effort, and genetics play a huge role in the potential to build strength and size.

Flexibility is developed in a very similar way. An athlete must stretch the muscles far enough to send a signal to the body that it needs to increase the length or elasticity of the muscles. Over time, the body will adapt to an aggressive flexibility program by creating a greater range of motion. This also takes quite a bit of time and effort, and genetics will determine an athlete's ultimate potential to increase flexibility. Not everyone will be able to do the splits, but it appears that implementing a stretching program can improve flexibility at any age. (The same is true for strength training in the development of strength.)

Because aggressive stretching can actually cause very small micro-tears in the muscles being stretched, it is generally recommended to do this *after* a training session. If a small tear is created before practice, it is possible that it could get worse during training and cause greater problems such as muscle pulls or strains. Therefore, a good warm up will focus on increasing the body's core temperature, moving the body in multiple planes, and will include some light stretching. The more productive (from a flexibility enhancement standpoint) and intense stretching should be done when the body will be able to recover from the micro-trauma, such as at the end of practice.

Another reason to stretch after activity is that it can increase the removal of waste products that accumulate during exercise, as well as increase the delivery of nutrients to the muscles. All of this helps in the recovery process which will ultimately decrease the potential for injury and improve performance.

Common Flexibility Issues

Tight Quadriceps or Hip Flexors: This can shorten stride length by limited the amount of knee flexion and hip extension the athlete is able to achieve. Short, choppy steps or an affected swing phase may be noticed during sprinting. The athlete may have trouble pulling the foot to the buttocks during the swing phase. Tenderness in the patellar tendon may also present itself in this situation.

An athlete should be able to pull his/her foot to the buttocks without too much effort. If this is difficult or impossible, quad stretches should be a priority.

Tight Achilles Tendon or Calf: This may present itself in a number of ways. Soreness in the Achilles tendon is common. You may also notice an inability to get into a full squat position or keep the feet pointing straight ahead while sprinting. While there may be other problems that are contributing to this, a lack of flexibility in the ankle may be the culprit.

If the ankle cannot dorsi-flex appropriately, the body will compensate by turning the foot outward while sprinting. Not only will this affect performance, it can also increase the risk of injury when done over a long period of time. Many athletes develop this habit early in life and assume that it is simply the way they move. Stretching the Achilles tendon and calf is relatively simple, but increasing flexibility in this area is sometimes challenging. Be sure to stress the importance of consistent work in this area to make a difference.

Tight Hamstrings: Everyone thinks they have tight hamstrings, but it is not as common as many people believe. If there is one area athletes stretch on a consistent basis, it is the hamstrings. Lying supine (face up), most athletes should be able to passively (someone pulling it up) pull a straight leg to at least 90°. This is just a guideline, and an inability to do this does not necessarily mean there is a problem.

Chapter 2 Coaching Tips

- Do not ever stretch a cold muscle as this may lead to injury. Your muscles are very similar to rubber bands. What do you think would happen if you put a rubber band in the freezer and then stretched it? It would be more likely to tear because it would be brittle and tight. The same thing occurs in your muscles. You are setting yourself up for injuries and will not enjoy all of the benefits if you stretch when you are cold.

- Take your time and do not force a stretch by bouncing or causing pain as this could lead to a soft tissue injury. During each stretch, slowly lengthen each muscle, gradually approaching the threshold of pain. It may feel a little uncomfortable, but should not be painful. If you stretch too quickly and/

or too far, safeguards within the nervous system will be activated and the benefits of the stretch will be lost. If you overstretch, slowly back off and let the muscle relax, then proceed with the stretch.

- If you are attempting to increase your flexibility, hold each stretch for 10-20 seconds and repeat two to three times, each time trying to go just a little further on the stretch. This can be done daily, and needs to be done consistently if improvements are expected. It is difficult to determine exactly how far you stretch a muscle each day, but over time, you should attempt to stretch farther than where you are at the beginning of your program. If increasing your flexibility is not a high priority, hold each stretch one time for 10-20 seconds, then move on to the next stretch.

- Not surprisingly, many of the most inflexible athletes are the laziest when it comes to stretching; they seem to resist performing any kind of consistent stretching routine. It is especially important for these athletes to stretch if performance is being hindered by a flexibility deficiency. A good coach will be able to recognize these needs and will be sure to make stretching a priority during practice.

- Coaches should always take the time to properly lead the warm-up and post-workout stretches. Too many coaches leave post-workout flexibility to the athletes without leading the stretches and ensuring that it is taken seriously. This kind of attitude teaches the athletes that stretching is not a priority and does not need to be taken seriously. They will quickly learn that stretching is unnecessary, so coaches must take this portion of practice seriously to demonstrate its importance to overall development.

The following pages contain several stretches for different muscles. There are many more stretches that are completely acceptable options. The stretches included here are good choices, and can form a complete program, but don't feel limited by them if you know of other stretches that are safe and effective for your situation.

Biceps

Chest

Upper Back

Shoulder

Triceps

Hip Flexors & Core

Abdominals

Glutes & Low Back

Quadriceps

Calves

Piriformis & Glutes

Glutes

Hamstrings & Calf

Groin

Chapter 3

Sprint Mechanics
&
Training Aids

In order for straight ahead speed to be developed, the foundation must be laid with proper sprinting mechanics. Once an athlete's mechanics are sound, additional training methods (strength training, plyometrics, weight vests, over-speed, sleds, etc.) can be incorporated. Without proper mechanics, additional training methods will yield less than optimal results.

The two basic factors involved in speed are:
- Stride length
- Stride frequency

Optimizing these two factors is the goal of any speed development program, but this is much easier said than done. The following information will help you gain a better understanding of sprint mechanics and some of the common technique errors. Also included are several drills to help correct each of these problems.

It will take a lot of practice for a coach to develop the ability to recognize mechanical errors, let alone choose and coach the appropriate drills to correct them. Take the time necessary to fully understand and analyze sprinting mechanics. Without the ability to analyze this complex movement and provide corrective feedback, a coach is of no use to an athlete trying to improve his/her speed. Also, keep in mind that there will be slight technique variations between athletes. While the technique described in this book is considered "optimal" by most experts, there are exceptions to the rule.

Olympic sprinting champion and World Record-holder Michael Johnson is a perfect example of individual variation in sprinting mechanics. Many coaches have remarked that Michael leans too far back while running. While this may be "true," it obviously hasn't had a negative impact on his speed. In fact, many athletes have considered leaning slightly backward because of his dominance.

There are many similar examples, and trying to change these exceptional athletes would probably cause more problems than it would be worth. But, for every amazingly gifted athlete who is the exception to the rule, there are thousands of "normal" athletes who will benefit from improved sprinting mechanics.

Does every athlete need to have perfect mechanics? Yes and no. Take an offensive lineman in football, for example. In a game situation, he may never run more than 10 yards in any play. Even during his short sprints, he will probably never open up and run in a way that improved top-end sprint mechanics would help. But, working on acceleration mechanics will certainly benefit this athlete, and if he is ever required to perform a 40-yard dash at a combine, sprint mechanics may be extremely important. Further, if the situation presents itself in a game situation where he needs to run fast, the time spent on running technique may pay huge dividends.

If a lineman can benefit from speed training, just about every other athlete in the world will benefit as well. Even a soccer goalkeeper, who doesn't typically cover a great deal of ground in a game, needs to have speed at his disposal when an important game situation makes it necessary. Because sprint training can benefit just about every athlete, it is important to understand the key concepts involved in teaching proper mechanics.

Arm Swing

Proper arm swing is extremely important to sprint speed, but many athletes have never been taught this motion. In fact, improper arm swing is one of the most common sprint technique errors, especially with younger athletes. Proper arm movement plays two very important roles:

1. Forceful backward swing of the arm assists the same-side leg to pull through to the high-knee position. If the arm is not pulled forcefully backward, it is more difficult for the knee to be properly driven forward on each step.
2. It also opposes the opposite-side knee drive, which keeps the spine and shoulders in alignment. The absence of the proper arm swing typically causes the spine and shoulders to rotate in an effort to maintain optimal pelvic positioning. Unfortunately, this creates a twisting motion which disturbs optimal functioning.

Figure 3.1 shows proper arm swing mechanics facing forward from a standing position, and Figure 3.2 illustrates proper form during sprinting.

Fig. 3.1 Arm Swing, Standing Front View

Fig 3.2 Arm Swing During Sprint

Elbows

To teach or learn proper arm swing, start in a standing position, legs slightly bent with a slight forward body lean. Bend elbows to approximately 90°. The elbows will stay bent at all times. The elbows will naturally bend to a slightly greater angle as they swing forward, and they will straighten slightly on the backswing. Allow this to happen naturally, but concentrate on keeping the elbows bent at 90° throughout the movement.

When initially instructed to bend and straighten the elbow slightly during the arm swing, many athletes will create too much movement at the elbow joint. A more experienced sprinter will be able to properly apply this feedback, but it is usually best to keep it simple when teaching proper mechanics to an athlete for the first time. Over-coaching may lead to confusion, so keep the coaching cues to a minimum when possible. Less information is easier to absorb and apply.

Hands & Wrists

The hands and wrists should be relaxed and free from excessive tension. Excessive tension in the hand and wrist will create tension all the way up the arm, and can inhibit the free motion required for optimal speed. Hand positioning can be determined by the individual as long as the hands are free of excessive tension. Figures 3.3 & 3.4 illustrate the most common hand positions, but deciding which position to use is ultimately a decision of personal preference.

Fig. 3.3 Light Fist

Fig. 3.4 Relaxed Open Hand

Arm Movement

The path in which the arms travel begins with the fingertips even with the chin or mouth (see Fig. 3.1). The hand should reach the mid-line of the body, but do not cross over that imaginary line. As you can see, the forearm will be on a slight angle. Be sure to keep the elbow bent at approximately 90° so the hand is several inches away from the face. (The number of inches will depend on individual limb length.)

The hand will then travel backward near the hip until it is slightly behind the hip. The hand should clear the hip at the end of the backswing (see Fig. 3.2). The elbows will stay relatively close to the body, but should not be squeezed inward too tightly. There should be limited lateral movement, as the athlete should focus on forward-backward movement, emphasizing the backward motion.

Common Problems

Unlike other aspects of sprint mechanics, the arm swing can be effectively practiced from a standing position without moving the feet. It also helps to have the athlete stand in front of a mirror while practicing the arm swing.

Upward Emphasis or Not Swinging Arms Back Far Enough, Fig 3.5: Have the athlete pretend that he/she is holding a hammer in each hand and pounding nails into a wall located directly behind him/her. Explain that the faster the arm is swung backward, the faster the leg will pull forward.

Shoulders Shrugged/Upper Back Tension, Fig 3.6: Have the athlete consciously relax the trapezius and shoulders to allow more natural free-flow movement. Practice in place looking in a mirror.

Side-to-Side Movement, Fig. 3.7: Practicing in front of a mirror can help an athlete understand what is happening so that excessive trunk rotation can be avoided.

Fig. 3.5 Arms not swinging back far enough

Fig. 3.6 Shoulders Shrugged

Fig. 3.7 Crossover Arm Swing

Leg Motion

While attention should be paid to proper arm movement, the motion of the lower body is far more important for developing speed. Obviously, the legs are doing most of the work while running and proper mechanics are crucial. Keep in mind, however, that there is a lot more room for error because of the complex nature of the lower body motion while sprinting. Take time to thoroughly understand lower-body mechanics and develop the ability to recognize faulty movement patterns. The following information will help you with this process, and more importantly, give you coaching tips to help correct common problems.

Knee Drive

The starting point for each step in a sprint is the knee drive position where the knee, hip, and ankle are all flexed in front of the body. The knees should be lifted much higher during sprinting than for slower running or jogging. The coach needs to emphasize a forceful, straight forward knee drive in order to place the leg in the optimal position for the downward/backward push of the sprinting motion. The angle of the hip in relation to the rest of the body should be approximately 70-80°. Typically, athletes do not have a high enough knee drive. It is rare to have an athlete actually drive his/her knees higher than necessary, so most of the coaching will be to encourage a more forceful knee drive. Fig. 3.8 shows proper knee drive position.

Common Problems

Cross Over, Fig 3.9: Some athletes will cross their knees inward over the mid-line of the body during knee drive. Explain that the legs are like the arms on a train locomotive; the arms travel in a straight path. You can also explain that it's like riding a bike; all of the movement is in one plane. This may take a lot of practice for some athletes and working in front of a mirror is helpful for the athlete to actually see what is happening.

Insufficient Knee Drive: As stated above, many athletes do not get their knees high enough. Often, it simply feels awkward to get the knees up because many athletes are accustomed to running with poor mechanics. This may take some time to feel natural, so be patient. It is also very likely that the athlete lacks strength in the hip flexors and abdominals. Weak abs will make it difficult to stabilize the pelvis, and weak hip flexors make it difficult to raise the thigh. Strength training will help alleviate these problems.

Fig 3.8 Knee Drive

Fig 3.9 Cross-over Knee Drive Exaggerated

Foot Strike & Support Phase

As the foot approaches the ground from the knee drive position, the ankle should be flexed in the toe-up (dorsiflexed) position, but the heel should never touch the ground. Athletes should be coached to stay on the balls of their feet without pointing the toes. The outside of the forefoot will make contact with the ground 0-6 inches in front of the body's center of mass. The foot should point directly forward and will land directly under the knee with the knee slightly flexed. The foot needs to be rigid as it hits the ground rather than "giving" as contact is made. This allows for optimal muscle recruitment in the lower leg, and allows power to be transferred efficiently from the upper leg through the foot.

Landing on the heels, or having the foot strike the ground in front of the knee, is like putting the brakes on; it will not allow for optimal sprinting performance. If foot strike occurs too far in front of the body in an effort to increase stride length, proper mechanics are lost, performance is negatively affected, and the potential for hamstring injury rises.

Fig. 3.10 Right foot just about to strike the ground under the COG

During acceleration (first 10-20 yards) the foot will strike the ground slightly behind the body's center of gravity (COG). The foot will strike well behind the COG for the first three steps and will gradually move forward as the athlete approaches maximal speed where a more upright posture is assumed. After the first 10-20 yards of a sprint, the foot will strike slightly in front of, or under, the COG. Fig. 3.10 shows foot strike while running at maximal (or near maximal) speed.

Common Problems

Cross Over: Many athletes will cross their feet over the mid-line of the body. To correct this, have the athlete run on a line and tell him/her to concentrate on keeping the feet on the sides of the line rather than crossing over. This may take a considerable amount of time and effort to correct and will feel rather awkward for the athlete. In addition to faulty neuromuscular programming, strength imbalances around the hip girdle can also contribute to this problem, so multi-directional strength should be assessed by a professional. This kind of testing is beyond the scope of this book, but coaches should be aware of this as a potential problem and should consider hip strengthening exercises for their athletes.

Toes Point Outward: Ask the athlete to simply point the feet forward, inward, and outward during easy runs. If they are capable of controlling these motions, there is a good chance that this is nothing more than a bad habit that will take a lot of concentration and practice to change the neural programming. If it is rather difficult for the athlete to control the motion, or if the athlete's knee, hip and ankle mechanics change considerably as the feet are pointed inward, forward and outward, there may be muscular or structural issues to deal with. Orthotics may help correct some of these problems. Other athletes may have deficiencies

Fig. 3.11 Fast Claw 1   **2**   **3**   **4**

in the lower leg or hip musculature that need to be addressed. Insufficient ankle flexibility may also contribute to this situation and can be addressed through a complete stretching program.

Over-striding: When instructed to take longer strides, many athletes plant the foot too far in front of the body's COG. This will be detrimental and can even be the cause of injuries. It will take some patience to correct this flaw. In addition to varying the coaching cues, teach the athlete the "Fast Claw" drill shown in Fig. 3.11 to help him/her understand the proper motion involved.

Under-striding: This will look like the athlete is taking short, choppy steps. This is typically an issue of improper mechanics and poor habits, but strength deficiencies in the hip are also common problems. Be careful to explain that lengthening the stride occurs by pushing off harder at toe-off, fully extending the hip, ankle and knee, and driving the knee forward to the high-knee position. When told to lengthen the stride, many athletes reach forward and foot-strike occurs in front of the knee, too far in front of the body's center of mass.

Fig. 3.12 Wall Push Drill

Landing on Heels: This can generally be corrected by simply making the athlete aware of what is occurring. Continue to give feedback and instruction until the athlete feels the proper motion. The High-Knees drill in the warm-up and Wall Push drill in Fig. 3.12 will usually get the athlete off the heels and can be used as a starting point for instruction.

Inward Kicking Motion at Toe-off: This is usually a motion that the athlete has no awareness of and can be difficult to correct. Treadmill running in a mirror is a good way to allow the athlete to actually see what is occurring. The Fast Claw drill can help the athlete keep the foot from kicking inward. Another technique is to have the athlete pretend his/her feet are on bicycle pedals which do not allow the foot to kick inward. This problem will typically be a long-standing habit developed at an early age and it will probably be necessary to begin with some very slow running with proper mechanics. When the task is mastered at a slow speed, gradually increase the pace until the athlete is properly executing at fast speeds. Shoe inserts or orthotics may also correct this problem if the feet are not functioning properly.

Ankle Plantar Flexed During Swing Phase: When athletes are told to "stay on the balls of the feet" many will plantar flex (point the foot) the ankle in an effort to stay off the heels. If the ankle is plantar flexed as it hits the ground, not only will it not be able to push off properly, but the anterior tibialis (shin muscles) will have to deal with a huge eccentric load during each step. This technique flaw needs to be addressed before major lower leg problems occur, but it can be very difficult for some athletes to make this change. Coach the athlete to pull the "toes toward knees" as soon as the foot leaves the ground during push off. Also, instruct the athlete to barely keep the heel from hitting the ground during the support phase. Many athletes mistakenly think they need to keep the heel as far off the ground as possible, so encourage them to keep it close to the ground without touching. Allow for many, sub-maximal speed repetitions to practice this. The Fast Claw drill is also a good way to address this problem. Also, use the high-knee and butt-kick drills with the ankle dorsi-flexed to reinforce the feeling of pulling the toes upward.

Foot Pronation/Eversion (ankle rolls inward/flat feet): Typically, the best way to correct this problem is through proper foot gear, shoe inserts, or orthotics. If you have a reputable specialty shoe store in your area, you *may* get good advice from an employee; this really depends on the knowledge of the employee. There are several off-the-shelf shoe inserts that alleviate many of the less severe problems. This may be the best first step to take. If the problem persists, even after the athlete has gone through the initial discomfort of adjusting to the inserts, the athlete may need the assistance of an orthotist to design a customized orthotic, or special exercises to improve the function of the foot. The diagnosis and possible solutions to this problem are extremely important if the foot is not functioning properly, but that process is beyond the scope of this book. Try to find a physical therapist, orthotist, or in some cases, athletic trainer or sports medicine physician, to address the problem.

Toe-Off & Swing Phase - Fig 3.13

As the foot leaves the ground during toe-off, the knee and ankle should be fully extended. A lack of full extension will shorten the stride and hinder optimal performance because the athlete is not fully utilizing the available musculature. This occurs very quickly, so it is rather difficult for a coach to see if this is actually happening. Often times it appears as though full extension is not happening at full speed, but slow motion video analysis reveals that it is indeed occurring. If you are at all unsure about this, video analysis can really help you see what is actually happening.

Fig. 3.13 Swing Phase (ankle will dorsiflex as it is pulled through)

The swing phase takes place as the foot is brought back to the front of the body in preparation for the next step. At toe-off, the hip is extended so that the foot is behind the body. As the swing phase begins, the knee bends and the foot is brought upward with the heel traveling toward the upper hamstrings or lower buttocks. The knee remains bent as the leg is pulled through to the "knee-up" position. It is important that the knee stays bent with the foot as close to the hamstrings as possible because this shortens the lever arm of the leg. If the knee is straight, the leg is essentially a longer lever that must be pulled through on each step. But, if the knee is bent, the lever arm shortens, and a shorter lever arm will travel faster than a long lever arm. This is basic physics applied in real life.

It is also important to have the ankle dorsiflexed (toe up position) during the swing phase and into the knee drive. A pointed toe (plantarflexed) position will create a longer lever and will put the foot and ankle in a very inefficient position at foot strike (see Foot Strike section). Athletes should be coached to dorsiflex the ankle as soon as the foot leaves the ground after toe-off. The ankle will not actually reach the dorsiflexed position until the foot passes under the body, but this happens so quickly that athletes should be coached to flex the foot as soon as it comes off the ground.

Common Problems

Not Getting Full Triple Extension: Try implementing some bounding drills that emphasize the full extension of the hip/knee/ankle. Place an emphasis on exaggerating stride length by driving the foot forcefully into the ground.

Foot Does Not Rise High Enough During Swing Phase: Tell the athlete to pretend he/she has a stick coming out of the inside of both knees. After the foot leaves the ground on each step, it needs to get over the stick during the knee drive. This will encourage the athlete to keep the knee bent during the swing phase and often helps to correct the problem.

Excessive Bounce: This is where the athlete's body bounces up and down during each step. This is wasted motion and increases the risk of injury while decreasing performance. Coach the athlete to keep the head and shoulders level while running. This is much easier to see if a mirror is present.

Pointed Foot During Swing Phase: As the foot leaves the ground at toe-off, some athletes will keep the foot pointed instead of flexing the foot upward. This will slow down the swing phase and will place the foot in an undesirable position to begin the knee drive. Coach the athlete to pull the toes toward the knees as soon as the foot leaves the ground. While many coaches will have athletes perform the "butt-kick" warm up drill with the feet and ankles pointed, it is a good idea to instruct the athlete to dorsiflex the ankle as it nears the buttocks just as it should during a sprinting motion. Performing the drill in this way can help an athlete get accustomed to properly executing this component of sprinting.

Active feet drills, or ankle flips, can also enhance foot/ankle action. This drill is like running, except with straight knees. The lower leg is responsible for the movement so the athlete can concentrate on pushing into the ground with the foot and flexing it again in preparation for the next step.

Pelvic Positioning

This is rather difficult for many coaches to assess, but it is crucial to the development of an optimal stride length. The pelvis can tilt forward or backward, see figures 3.13 & 3.14. The optimal pelvic alignment during sprinting is 2-6° of forward tilt. A forward tilt of greater than 6° will make it difficult to execute proper knee drive, and a backward tilt of the pelvis will limit hip extension and negatively affect stride length. Some athletes have poor posture and an abnormal pelvic tilt feels natural.

Common Problems

Anterior (forward) pelvic tilt: Many athletes seem to "stick their butts out," and appear to be falling forward when they sprint. This is often due to an excessive forward pelvic tilt. Tight hip flexors and low back musculature is often the culprit. Poor postural habits can also be the cause. Evaluate the athlete's flexibility and test their ability to control the pelvic girdle. If there is a lack of control, transverse abdominal awareness may be compromised or there could simply be a lack of body awareness.

Have the athlete pretend his/her pants are full of water. Without moving the rest of the body, ask him/her to pour the water out the front of the pants, then the back of the pants. He/she should be able to control this movement. A homework assignment could be to practice this movement until greater control is achieved. You can also stand the athlete with his/her head, butt, and heels against a wall. Without moving anything else, ask him/her to draw in the abdominals and push the lower-back against the wall. Working on this is another good homework assignment. Awareness of the pelvic girdle will often lead to greater control. And, greater control may allow the athlete to make the necessary adjustments while sprinting.

Fig 3.13 Posterior (backward) pelvic tilt

Fig 3.14 Anterior (forward) pelvic tilt

Acceleration

While top-end speed is important in certain situations, the ability to rapidly accelerate is arguably the most important physical predictor of athletic success. For years, University of Nebraska strength and conditioning coaches have been telling us that, through years of data collection, they have found that the single most important predictor of athletic success is the 10 yard dash – in other words, the ability to accelerate.

Further research shows that maximal strength in the gluteus and quads plays a major role in the ability to accelerate (the hamstrings play a much larger role in top-end speed). As strength improves, so does the ability to accelerate. Yet, you only use a small percentage of your maximal strength in most activities. Some experts say that only about 30% of maximal strength is actually used when performing high-velocity motions such as sprinting. It seems that more than 30% of maximal strength is probably used during the initial phase of rapid acceleration or during directional changes. Whatever the percentage, the point is that the greater your maximal strength, the greater your 30% (or whatever percentage it actually is) ends up being. So, increasing your maximal strength is a part of speed, but there is certainly more to the equation.

Most athletes reach about 80% of their top-end speed around 20 yards into a sprint. World class sprinters are able to accelerate longer and typically have a much higher top-end speed than other athletes. It is interesting to note, however, that most world class athletes are not world class sprinters and they don't have world class top-end speed. What they have is the ability to reach their top speed extremely quickly.

It is important to have good starting mechanics for a timed sprint, but true acceleration in sports usually does not begin from a complete stop. It is critical for an athlete to able to accelerate while already moving, or to "hit another gear." This ability is what allows athletes to get to a loose ball, close the gap, drive the lane, hit an open hole, or create separation.

A running back often must start slowly, wait for the line to open a hole, then accelerate quickly through the hole with a burst of speed. Soccer players are typically in motion when the need to accelerate to a ball presents itself. Tennis players generally take 3-6 steps in order to make a shot. An explosive basketball player usually takes less than six steps in a drive to the basket. Top end speed makes no difference to performance, but those first few steps are crucial.

The mechanics involved in acceleration are very different than distance running. They are even different than top-end sprinting mechanics. Why, then, do so many coaches require athletes to log mile after mile in an effort to prepare for competition? It doesn't make sense. For just about every sport, other than distance running, athletes are much better served practicing the ability to accelerate as quickly as possible. The neuromuscular requirements involved in rapid acceleration are unique and need to be trained exactly the way they will be used.

Fig. 3.15 Forward lean during acceleration

When accelerating, the head and shoulders need to be in front of the center of gravity (COG) and the foot should strike the ground well behind the COG. This is important so the force being put into the ground allows the body to accelerate horizontally. If you are standing erect while attempting to accelerate, your feet will drive downward into the ground. Simple physics tells us that if you push straight down into the ground, the force will create an opposite (or upward) motion. But, if your feet are pushing backward behind your COG, the force now propels you forward. Fig. 3.15 shows the forward lean necessary to accelerate quickly.

When accelerating from a standstill, most athletes understand this concept, and the same concept applies to accelerating while already moving. While jogging, the body will naturally be upright. When a burst of speed is called for, a forward lean is necessary to initiate the acceleration. This lean is what allows the feet to drive backward into the ground behind the COG. This concept may seem simple (and it is), but it needs to be correctly practiced in order to become a natural movement sequence than can be utilized in competition. The simple drill of jogging 10 yards, then accelerating 10 yards can be modified by accelerating from a shuffle, backpedal, skip, or crossover run. This is covered in more depth in the Transition Movement section of this book.

Speed-Enhancement Products

The research on speed development reveals that increasing the force created by each step, thus improving stride length, plays a much greater role than attempting to increase stride frequency. With this in mind, several training devices/techniques have been developed to enhance this important aspect of speed.

Fig 3.16 Weight vest

Weighted Vests/Shorts, Fig 3.16 – There is some scientific literature that suggests wearing a weighted vest with a very small load (1-3% of bodyweight) can help optimize the body's ability to rapidly produce force in the specific movement patterns utilized in sport performance. Because the resistance is low, the movement velocity and mechanics do not change. When used over time, the body may learn to produce more force when performing the practiced movements. Contrast training (performing some reps with the vest and some without) is recommended to optimize the nervous system's opportunity to adapt to the load. Always perform a few reps without the vest after practicing with it on, and be sure to choose a vest that fits snuggly and conforms to your body, to minimize shifting during training. Overall, a weighted vest will probably not have a negative effect on performance, and there is a good chance that it can have a positive effect. Agility drills and conditioning can also be done with a good vest.

Parachutes – Although they have become a popular training device, very little research has been done on parachutes. Theoretically, the resistance will create a more forceful extension of the hip during the sprinting motion. Results will vary greatly depending on the size and strength levels of the athlete. Certain athletes may be able to use a chute correctly, while many others will see their mechanics change dramatically because of the resistance. Good coaching is essential if a chute is to be used effectively. Overall, parachutes have the potential to have a negative effect on performance if used incorrectly, but the risk is minimal. On the other hand, the chances of a parachute actually improving speed is questionable with beginner- or intermediate-level athletes. Advanced trainees will probably get the most out of training with a parachute. An experienced coach is a must.

Over-speed/Towing Devices – There is some validity to using over-speed training in an effort to increase stride frequency. The problem with this method is that it is not very practical and may be somewhat harmful. Many tubing devices that claim to utilize the principles of over-speed training never really get an athlete up to a speed greater than he/she is capable of. Towing behind a car can certainly push an athlete past his/her capabilities, but this is a very unsafe practice and is not recommended. Training on a high speed treadmill is probably the safest and most practical way to do this, but very few people have access to a treadmill capable of appropriate speeds. In addition, the arms cannot be used, body lean may change, and it is still somewhat dangerous to jump on a treadmill going that fast. Can over-speed training help increase stride frequency? Perhaps. The research in this area is inconclusive. Can it be dangerous? Yes. Should you use it? It may be useful for some athletes to use this method infrequently, but it is certainly not a requirement for speed development.

Sleds – As long as the load is relatively light, sleds have the potential to be an effective training device, especially when training for acceleration or an explosive start. The concern is that mechanics may be compromised, so using a relatively light weight and having a good coach are essential to ensure proper technique is used. Like a weighted vest, contrast training is recommended to ensure the nervous system practices with and without the load. Sleds are also a great way to add resistance to backpedal work.

Resistance Tubing – There are a plethora of resistance tubing devices available that all claim to improve speed. While some of them may be beneficial, most of these devices have limited merit. For agility training, there are devices that include a tube attached to a belt around the waist. With this device, athletes can perform movement in all directions without altering footwork or mechanics. This device may be beneficial, but it is very coach intensive since only one person can use the device while a coach needs to hold the tube. Obviously, there are creative ways of making this happen, so don't let this limit you. Be careful with some of the other devices that may seriously alter movement mechanics.

Special Shoes, or shoe attachments that elevate the fore foot – Studies on these shoes have shown they do not work, and may be dangerous. The studies showed no difference between training with or without the special shoes, but concluded that there is an increased risk of ankle and Achilles tendon injury due to the awkward nature of the shoe and the altered movement mechanics used when wearing them. Not recommended.

Weighted Jumps – Several studies have shown that performing jumps with 30% of your maximal squat load maximizes mechanical power output and can contribute to speed development. While jumping with a loaded bar on your back can be dangerous, there are alternatives. Holding dumbbells at your side will eliminate some of the compressive forces on the spine and allow the athlete to drop the weights if necessary. Performing the jumps on specialized machines is an excellent alternative if available, and a heavily loaded weight vest may be a good option. All of these modalities are excellent alternatives to performing Olympic weightlifting movements.

Incline Running – Incline running has been shown through force platforms to elicit much greater propulsive forces than running on flat surfaces. The two concerns involved with incline running are that the athlete will slow down because of the decreased stride frequency and that running mechanics will change. Proper coaching can easily eliminate both of these problems, but everyone should be aware of these concerns before engaging in an incline running program. It is also important to contrast the incline running with some flat surface sprints to maximize the transfer to ground running. Many of the most successful athletes of all time, including Jerry Rice and Walter Payton, talked about incline sprinting as an important part of their speed and conditioning programs. Fig. 3.17 shows an example of incline running on a high-power treadmill.

Decline Running – Decline running is similar to towing or overspeed training and can be beneficial if used properly. A very small decline of 1-5° should be used. Even this slight decline can alter mechanics, but a greater decline has the potential to drastically affect movement technique and can place a great deal of stress on the joints. Decline running should be used sparingly and only with properly trained athletes. Be sure to contrast decline running with flat surface running to maximize the potential impact it can have on running speed.

Fig. 3.17 Incline Treadmill Running

Treadmill Running, Fig. 3.17 – There has been some controversy and misinformation surrounding treadmill running for speed development. When the first research on the transfer of treadmill running to over-ground running began, the studies used standard "health club" treadmills at jogging speeds. Some of the studies determined that treadmill running was identical to over-ground running, and some of the studies determined that they were different. Subsequent studies utilized a much different kind of treadmill with extremely large flywheels and a powerful motor. This treadmill also had a force platform built into the deck which measured both horizontal and vertical ground forces. This research showed that the "beefed-up" treadmill was very different than a "health club" model and that the ground reaction forces were identical to over-ground running.

It has also been suggested that treadmill running is different than over-ground running because the belt somehow pulls the foot through on each step. This argument defies logic because each step on a treadmill obviously must create enough horizontal force to keep the body in place on the deck. If the foot was actually "pulled through," backward movement would occur, and the exerciser would fall off the treadmill. Instead, the exerciser must put enough force into the treadmill to stay in one place on the moving belt.

Treadmill sprinting can be a very effective way to work on mechanics, incorporate incline training, and push an athlete through fatigue for optimal conditioning. Along with a mirror in front of the athlete, a good treadmill sprinting program is an excellent way to work on sprinting mechanics. It is very easy for a coach to analyze the sprinting mechanics on a treadmill because the athlete is right in front of him/her. For the athlete, the ability to receive feedback while sprinting at top speed is invaluable, especially with a mirror that allows him/her to see what is actually happening. No matter how you feel about treadmill running, the right treadmill can be an amazing tool if used properly. It appears that standard treadmills found in most health clubs are not appropriate for sprint training, but the "beefed up" treadmills made by a couple of manufacturers create horizontal and vertical ground forces identical to over-ground running.

Footgear

Many people have poorly functioning feet, but the diagnosis and treatment of these problems is underestimated and often misunderstood. Just about every movement we make in sports starts with the feet, so it's crucial to have properly functioning feet with appropriate foot gear. A poorly functioning foot has the potential to cause problems at the knee, hip, and low back, and may create difficulties with the mechanics of many athletic movements. The proper shoe can help alleviate many of these problems, and can actually help many athletes move more efficiently. Unfortunately, athletic foot gear has become a study in fashion and aesthetics; functionality and durability, the most important aspects of a shoe, are often overlooked.

In a world dominated by marketing campaigns and driven by the dollar, many shoes look great, but just don't perform well. In the shoe world, it's easy to trick consumers into buying a lousy shoe when they look flashy and have a famous athlete's name on them. That is enough to sell a lot of shoes, but don't be the fool. There are a lot of good shoes to choose from if you know what to look for.

Each shoe company has at least a few decent shoes in their line, but some brands seem to produce superior shoes for athletic performance. They produce diverse lines of shoes so different foot types can get an excellent fitting shoe. Many podiatrists recommend New Balance shoes to their patients because of the individualized fit and excellent function available in many of their products, but there are certainly other companies that build quality shoes.

Like coaching speed and agility, you need a good "coach" to help you find the right shoe for your foot. A good shoe salesperson should understand the differences in each shoe and should be able to recommend the right product for your particular situation. If you are lucky enough to live in an area with a high quality athletic shoe store nearby, there is a good chance that the employees will be able to properly fit you with a shoe that will optimize the function of your foot.

There are many small shoe stores or chains that have employees who are able to fit you with the appropriate shoe, so I encourage you to look for a store in your area where you can get the kind of service you need. Some of these stores actually train their employees on the materials and design intricacies of each shoe available in the store. Many shoe manufacturers create shoes to fit the needs of different foot conditions, so it's important to deal with an employee that understands the intended use of each shoe. For example, some shoes are made to help control over-pronation (this looks like fallen arches) and some are made to control supination (the opposite of over-pronation where too much weight is placed on the outside of the foot). If you have a fairly normal foot, and mistakenly purchase a shoe that is intended to correct supination, this could cause some serious discomfort or even injury depending on the way you use the shoe. Having a knowledgeable salesperson can help you find the right shoe for your foot, especially if you have foot problems. You can certainly find quality shoes in "big box" stores, but it is more common to find knowledgeable salespeople at a smaller, specialized store.

If your shoe isn't made for your particular foot and the activities in which you will be using it, you are simply not going to be able to perform as safely or effectively as possible. For multi-directional agility work, look

Fig. 3.18 Fold Test. The forefoot should be flexible while the arch remains rigid.

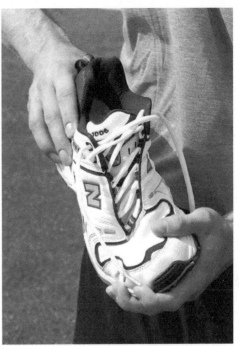

Fig. 3.19 Twist Test. Shoe should resist excessive twisting.

for a shoe with a low profile and plenty of lateral support. The material will be relatively rigid (such as leather), and you should not be able to bend the shoe at the point where the arch support is located. Fig. 3.18 shows the "fold test" to evaluate the material supporting the arch. Well supported shoes will also resist the "twist test" shown in Fig. 3.19. These shoes are typically called Cross-Trainers, and many stores have a separate area for them.

Basketball and court shoes will have many similarities. The twist and fold tests are a good start for both of these purposes. Basketball shoes will typically have a high-top or mid-rise profile for increased ankle support. Many basketball players tape their ankles anyway, which will provide additional support. The main difference in a court shoe will be leather on the top of the toes which is simply there because many racquet sports use movements that drag the toe. The extra material simply guards against holes worn in the top of shoes because of this toe dragging motion. Court shoes are typically not high-tops, but there is no real reason why a high-top could not be used for racquet sports.

Running shoes are generally not appropriate choices for intense agility work because of the lack of lateral support, the relatively high profile, and the light-weight material used to make them comfortable for distance running. One common mistake people make when choosing a shoe is picking the cushiest one available; many people want to feel like they're walking on pillows. But, if the shoe is too cushy, your foot will not be able to properly react to the ground during athletic movement. The cushy sole feels great when you try it on, but for running or agility work, that cushy feel is quite inappropriate. A shoe with a thick sole or light material on the sides will also put you at a greater risk for ankle injury if you're doing any lateral agility work. These shoes will allow your foot to move around inside them, not allowing for optimal function during a change of direction.

As you can see in fig. 3.20, even an extremely high quality shoe takes a beating during a change of direction. The shoe in this picture is a well designed model for lateral support, using heavier material on the lateral aspect of the shoe to support the foot during cutting motions. You can see how the foot shifts inside the shoe and puts tremendous pressure on the material. If a typical running shoe were worn, there would be less lateral support and the foot would slide off the sole even more than seen here. The sole on a running shoe may also be thicker, increasing the potential for the foot to slide off and injure the ankle.

Fig. 3.20 Lateral shoe support during foot plant

Athletic cleats are also a huge part of many sports including soccer, football, rugby, baseball and lacrosse. When the playing surface is grass, a cleated shoe will provide much better traction than a smooth soled shoe, which will lead to much better stopping, starting, and directional changes. The two most common problems with cleats are inappropriate spike lengths and bulky, boot-like shoes.

The spike length of a cleat is dependent on the condition of the field, and it is often appropriate to have different cleats for different conditions. If the grass is very long and wet, a long-spiked, screw-in cleat is appropriate. These cleats will sink into the ground better and will not pack mud between the spikes as easily. If the grass is relatively short and dry, a shorter spike is much more appropriate and will give you better traction. A turf shoe may be the best choice if the grass is very short and/or dry.

A bulky, boot-like shoe is simply not necessary anymore with the quality of shoes available. A heavy or bulky shoe will inevitably hinder performance and will not provide any better traction than a more form fitting shoe. There are several all-leather cleats or turf shoes that are light, form fitting, and will not detract from performance. There is no reason to train diligently to improve your speed and agility if you are going to wear a heavy shoe that slows you down.

Many young athletes also tend to wear their shoes or cleats very loosely. A loosely tied shoe is not only a complete waste of material, it will also slow you down and can be very dangerous when performing athletic movements. Your foot may slide around inside the shoe and lead to an ankle injury if this happens during a hard cut or plant. If your foot is flopping around inside the shoe, you will not be able to deliver as much force into the ground as possible. Select a shoe that properly fits your needs, and lace them up every time you plan to participate in events that require rapidly changing directions.

People with pronated feet (fallen arches) should look for a shoe with very solid material used at the arch. The arch support in the sole should not bend during a "fold test," and you will feel a noticeable buildup of material at the arch to help control the pronation. This is an extremely common issue, and many shoe companies have responded by offering appropriate models in their line.

Many foot problems can be lessened through foot-strengthening routines, but most people are simply unwilling to dedicate themselves to correcting mild problems, especially when shoes are available that seem to alleviate their symptoms. While this does not necessarily fix the problem, wearing the right shoe is a good place to start.

The next step is to use an insert that has arch support and a heel cup such as in Fig. 3.21. There are several companies that offer these very inexpensive ($10-25) items, and the benefits are incredible for many people. In fact, for many people, an inexpensive insert will correct up to 90% of the deficiencies that an expensive, custom made orthotic will. Many physical therapists and orthotists will tell you that most people could benefit in some way from a decent insert, and that the inserts will do nothing but help; they generally will not exacerbate any problems so there seems to be no real risk in experimenting with them, especially if you're feet aren't functioning optimally.

Fig. 3.21 Basic arch support and heel cup

You can find quality inserts at many good shoe stores, and a lot of physical therapy clinics now carry these items for their patients. Just as with selecting a shoe, it is recommended that you ask for assistance when selecting your insert to be sure you are using the best design for your situation.

Chapter 3 Coaching Tip

The movements involved in speed and agility work are very complex. Because they are complex, it is appropriate to break them down into more manageable movements that can be worked on separately. Keep in mind, however, that any portion of a movement that is worked on separately must always be integrated back into the whole skill to be effective.

Athletes can get overwhelmed with information if you have them work on every single aspect of the movement all at once. When there is too much to think about, results will be limited. So, try to pick one or two points to work on each session so progress can be made more efficiently.

Always keep in mind that, while developing a skill, quality is much more important than quantity. This is particularly true when working on linear speed. Keep the workouts brief with a high level of intensity, and focus energy on technique.

Notes

Chapter 4

Explosive Starts

Not including a track start from blocks (which is only useful in track meets and will not be covered in this book) there are four basic starting positions:

1. 3-Point Start
2. Standing Start
3. Athletic Position
4. Moving Start/Transition Movement

While there are certainly variations on these starting positions, working from these positions will enable an athlete to feel comfortable in almost any situation in which he/she must accelerate rapidly.

When working on starting technique, try to keep your athletic goals in mind. If you're going to be tested on the 40-yard dash, for example, an excellent 3-Point Start is crucial to your success. If, however, your goal is to excel on the field or court, it is not necessary to spend nearly as much time on this technique. All of the starts have similarities, but be sure to focus your time and energy practicing the skills used most often in your sport.

3-Point Start & 40-Yard Dash

Although it will never be used in any competitive sport situation, the 3-Point Start is the best choice when performing a timed sprint such as the 40-yard dash. When used properly, it helps put the athlete in a position that takes full advantage of the forward lean so crucial to acceleration. From the forward lean position, an athlete is able to generate maximal horizontal force, which will elicit the greatest propulsive power possible.

When executed poorly, however, the 3-Point Start has the potential to negatively impact a sprint time. Initially, it may feel rather awkward for many athletes, so it is important to dedicate plenty of practice time to master the skill if it is going to be used. With so much riding on the tests at football combines, it would behoove any athlete who may get tested to spend time perfecting this technique. A good start will make or break a 40- yard dash, so practice is vital.

To begin, place the dominant leg forward, with the toes approximately six inches behind the starting line as in Fig. 4.1. The dominant leg is typically the one you would jump off for a long jump or to dunk a basketball. Whichever foot you would naturally kick a soccer or football with will be placed in the back. This is not an absolute, but it is a very common way to

Fig. 4.1 Sprint start preparation

determine the starting position. Most athletes will place the left foot forward.

The back foot will be placed at hip-to-shoulder width, with the toes of the back foot even with the heel of the front foot. Squat down on the balls of the feet, and place one hand on the ground even with the starting line (Fig. 4.2). The hand placed on the ground will be from the same side of the body as the back foot. The hand will be placed on the ground perpendicular to the direction of the sprint, and most of the weight will be placed on the thumb and first two fingers, as in Fig. 4.2.

At this point in the preparation phase of the start, the opposite hand will be on the ground about a foot ahead of the starting line. This hand will be used to balance the body and will help place you in a good forward lean position before take-off. Straighten the knees slightly to assume a more upright position and rock the body forward so there is weight equally distributed on the hands and feet. A great deal of weight will be placed on the front hand at this point, but it will be removed before take-off to ensure a legal start.

Fig. 4.2 Sprint start hand placement. Note hand placement of right hand. Left hand is used for balance in this picture.

In this starting position, both knees will be bent at approximately 90°, with the front leg bent slightly more than the back leg. The weight will be placed onto the balls of the feet, and there should be weight on both feet. The head will be down at this point, with the eyes looking straight down or a few feet in front of the starting line.

Just before take-off, the hand in front of the starting line will be pulled back to a position behind the body with the elbow bent slightly, as in Fig. 4.3. Now that the hand has been taken off the ground, you will only be able to balance in this position for about one second before you will begin falling forward. To begin accelerating, rip the back arm forward at the same time you drive off of both feet. It will almost feel as though you are jumping forward with both feet, but the back knee will drive forward. Take a powerful step and land on the ball of the foot. Of course, most of the power will come from the front foot, so any additional force that can be generated from the back leg will add to the forward propulsion.

Full extension of the hip, knee and ankle of the front leg should be accomplished before it comes through for its first step, as in Fig 4.4. Just before the front leg takes its first step, the body should be extended in a straight line from head to toe, with the

Fig 4.3 Starting position just before take off

"back" arm driving forward. The body should be leaning forward as far as possible without falling over. The second and third steps should be driven into the ground as hard as possible to maximize acceleration. Many people do not get optimal acceleration from each of the first three steps, so continue practicing this until it feels natural.

A good forward lean position is a little hard to get used to because it feels as though you are going to fall on your face. It is absolutely imperative that the knees drive hard so you don't trip and fall. It is also a good coaching cue to tell the athlete to push backward into the ground as hard as possible with each step. Some coaches tell their athletes to rip the turf up behind them in an effort to put as much force into the ground as possible. The gluteus and quadriceps are responsible for most of this propulsion.

Pushing forcefully into the ground will also give the "swing" leg enough time to drive forward for the next step. If the "swing" leg does not make it far enough forward before it touches down to the ground, you will feel like you are tripping or falling forward. This will knock you off-balance and will really slow you down.

As you gain speed, the body will slowly rise to a more upright position. By 10-15 yards the body will be close to upright, and by 20 yards most athletes will only have a 2-6° forward lean. At this point (about 20 yards) most athletes will have achieved 80-90% of their top-end speed, and will be utilizing full-stride sprint mechanics. The hamstrings are much more active in this phase of sprinting as the leg is pulled forcefully backward on each step.

The stride-length will gradually increase during the sprint, while stride-frequency should be maintained. Maintaining a fast stride frequency while increasing the stride-length is the ultimate goal when attempting to increase top speed. Increasing the stride length must be done by increasing the propulsive force of each step, rather than over-striding and changing mechanics. It is also important that the sprint be finished at top speed, so be sure to sprint hard all the way through the finish line.

Fig. 4.4 First step from a 3-point start

Standing Start - Fig. 4.5

The Standing Start is a much more realistic starting position for most sports. While it is rare in competition to take off from a pre-determined starting position and run in a straight line, it is much more realistic that starting from a 3-Point Start position.

The Standing Start is very similar to the 3-Point Start, except you will not crouch down as low or place your hand on the ground. Your feet will be set up the same as in the 3-Point Start, but your knees will have less of a bend before take-off. Unlike the picture, you can move the front foot all the way up to the starting line if being timed. Your front hand will be hanging loosely in front of you, while the back hand will be cocked back at your side. The back arm will really help generate momentum from this position because the legs will not be able to create as much horizontal propulsion as in the 3-Point Start. Try to lean forward as far as possible before take-off to get the maximum forward lean from this position.

Try to push off both feet like in the 3-Point Start, but the back foot will do very little work front this position. Instead, focus on taking powerful steps during acceleration, and create a forward lean for the first 5-10 yards. It is a good idea to begin falling slightly forward just before take off to make this happen.

It is also very tempting to take a "false step" from this position. While the false step may not be nearly as bad as we once thought, it is unnecessary from this position and should be avoided. Be sure to keep your weight forward on the balls of the feet, and pick up the back foot to take the first step.

Fig. 4.5 Standing Start

Athletic Position and False Step - Fig. 4.6 & 4.7

The most important aspect of this start is to get into a good athletic position with the feet wide and a good bend in the knees to keep the body low. Slightly different from the standard "ready position," it is recommended to have the feet slightly staggered to allow for better forward and backward movement than in a "parallel feet" position. This position will allow for optimal movement in any direction – forward, backward, and laterally – without the need for adjustment.

The staggered-step positioning appears to be an excellent "ready position" for many sports, and its use is recommended in many situations because of its versatility. Many athletes such as baseball outfielders, football defensive backs, soccer defenders, martial artists and tennis players already utilize the staggered-step position because it allows for balanced movement in any direction. In one-on-one situations like football pass coverage or basketball "on-ball" defense, the staggered-step position also allows the defensive player to cheat to one side in an attempt to force the offensive player to one direction. This tactic helps the defensive player dictate some of the movement and lessens the advantage of the offensive player.

Because one foot is already dropped slightly backward, the use of the "false step" is significantly altered. Once considered a counterproductive motion, recent research has shown that the "false step" is actually not detrimental to overall speed from a "parallel-feet" ready position. The false step is simply a small step backward which allows for a forward lean and puts the body in a position to drive the feet backward into the ground to create forward propulsion. Many coaches see this backward step as wasted movement and encourage athletes not to use this technique. Interestingly, research on this movement pattern revealed that while the initial step backward does take slightly longer to initiate forward movement, the false step actually generates more power in the first 2-3 steps and allows the athlete to accelerate faster than other techniques. The end result is that the false step seems to get athletes to their destination as fast, if not faster, than other techniques.

Fig. 4.6 Traditional athletic position

Fig. 4.7 Staggered-step athletic position

While the research on different movement patterns is not always helpful, this research seems to reinforce the "natural" technique that many athletes seem to utilize when starting from a "parallel-feet" position. By placing the feet in a slightly staggered position to begin with, the need for the backward "false step" is eliminated at the same time you take advantage of this powerful movement technique; you are already in an optimal position for acceleration, so the extra step is unnecessary.

From the new staggered-step Athletic Position, it is important to initiate movement with the outside foot while taking the first step with the inside foot. This is very similar to the technique utilized in a change of direction, which is covered in Chapter 5. Because the footwork involved is identical, practicing agility movements will make this a more comfortable movement pattern, and vice versa.

Transition Movement

Although Transition Movement is used more in competition than any other acceleration technique it is drastically under-practiced. Transition Movement, as the name suggests, transitions from one movement or speed to another movement or speed. Although it does not begin from a complete standstill as the other starts do, it is being discussed as a "start" because of the strong acceleration component involved. Transition Movement is used in just about every sport, and the ability to accelerate while already moving seems to be a huge determinant for overall athletic success.

Imagine a football running back taking a hand-off and looking for a hole. At this point, the RB is moving but he is not fully accelerating yet. Once the hole is located, the RB shifts to another gear and accelerates as quickly as possible. This is one example of a moving start. Another example is a soccer player jogging into position when the ball is suddenly kicked within a few yards of her. From the jog, she needs to accelerate to maximum speed as quickly as possible to win the ball. There are numerous examples of this, and it is unnecessary to list them all. The point is that accelerating while in motion occurs all the time in sports and is a huge part of athleticism. Unfortunately, many coaches focus only on the first three starts listed, and never practice Transition Movement.

Because of its importance and common usage, it is recommended that Transition Movement be practiced from a variety of positions. In competitive situations, the athlete will not always be moving in the same direction when acceleration needs to occur, so drills need to be created to allow for different movements and directions. Many of the cone drills are appropriate for this type of transition from one movement to another. It is also very important that athletes attempt to accelerate as quickly as possible when practicing these transitions. When practicing any change of direction (COD), athletes should be coached to accelerate hard out of the directional change. This will help develop explosive transitions between movements.

The footwork involved here will vary greatly between the different movement transitions, but there are two common aspects to look for. First, a forward body lean should be created whenever an athlete is attempting to accelerate. Simply leaning the entire body forward in the intended direction is all that needs to occur to help facilitate acceleration. This sounds very simple, but many young athletes do not understand this concept. Like any other sport fundamental, this needs to be taught to young athletes to ensure that they understand how body positioning helps control movement. This forward lean creates an optimal body position to apply force into the ground.

The second common aspect is to keep the feet wide, lower the body's center of mass, and plant with the outside foot if the acceleration occurs after a COD. Chapter 5 provides more details on proper directional-change mechanics and will help coaches and athletes understand the footwork involved.

Chapter 4 Coaching Tip

Because acceleration is such a vital part of most sports, plan on devoting a significant amount of practice time to developing this trait. Always explain that a drill is intended to work on acceleration and that adequate rest periods will be given between sets. During speed and agility training, some athletes will simply try to *get through* the workout rather than giving 100% intensity on each drill. While this kind of *pacing* may get an athlete through a workout, it will never allow for optimal speed development. If the athletes understand that this particular portion of the workout is not "conditioning" work, they will be much more willing to give 100% on each repetition.

Of course, it is up to the coach to keep the drills fresh and always allow plenty of time to recover between sets. Athletes may actually seem a little bored, but it is important to explain what they are working on, why they are resting so much and that performing the acceleration drills with sub-maximal effort will severely limit the training benefits.

When you notice an athlete giving sub-maximal effort, talk to him/her about how the nervous system will never learn how to perform optimally if the athlete does not consistently give maximal effort. It is also useful to ask the athlete why maximal effort is not being given.

An example of what to say is, "It looks to me like you're not running as fast as you possibly can. I think you are capable of more. Is there a reason you are not pushing yourself right now?"

This puts the responsibilty on the athlete, and forces him/her to think about why 100% effort is not being given. Asking this question is also a good idea because there may actually be something limiting the athlete. There could be an injury or emotional issue that needs to be addressed, and the only way to find out is by asking a simple question. If done tactfully, without demeaning the athlete, this kind of discussion will also tell the athlete that you care and want the best for him/her.

If the athlete tells you there is nothing wrong and has no reason for the lack of effort, consider asking whether or not he/she wants to improve. If the answer is "no," a more in-depth discussion needs to take place. If, however, the answer is "yes," then all of the responsibility falls on the athlete's shoulders. If the behavior continues, you can remind him/her of your conversation and explain that the lack of effort is not acceptable.

When these steps have been taken, athletes are apt to give excellent effort on each drill, thus enhancing the training benefits.

Chapter 5

Lightning-Quick Agility

In general, agility is most useful in sports that emphasize open-loop skills (see Chapter 1 for a discussion on open- vs. closed-loop skills). Quick changes of direction are typically used to evade or defend an opponent, or react to a situation during competition. The principles outlined in this chapter focus on the fundamental skills used in these situations. Yes, there are fundamental agility skills; and while there are many variations, practicing these fundamental movements will boost any athlete's overall athleticism.

The agility mechanics described in this chapter are geared toward proper execution during competition, not for testing purposes. The skills involved in combine-type testing are unique to each drill and need to be practiced specifically to improve performance on these tests. This kind of testing assumes that superior performance in closed-loop skills will translate to success in open-loop skills. This is not always an accurate assumption, but the reality of the situation is that many coaches weigh these tests very heavily when evaluating talent. With this in mind, it is important to enhance both real-life agility (which will be addressed here) as well as testing efficiency on particular drills, which differs greatly from many game situations.

Proper agility mechanics are typically not taught to young athletes, so this is an area that can often make a huge difference to a competitive athlete. For many athletes, working on proper agility mechanics is met with resistance. Much like changing sprinting mechanics, the new movement patterns are often uncomfortable and feel like they are slowing the athlete down. Initially, this may indeed occur as the athlete will go through a transition period before the new movements feel natural and can be used effectively in competitive situations. But, like improving sprinting mechanics, it is worth the effort and will ultimately allow an athlete to perform as close to optimally as possible.

Because open-loop agility is greatly dependent upon the actions of an opponent or unpredictable game situations, you can imagine that there is a huge variety of movements that can be made. With this in mind, there are several common components of agility that are typically, but not always, utilized. Understand that these components are not *always* utilized because of the complex nature of reacting to different external stimuli.

Physical abilities will also determine the repertoire of movement options that each athlete has access to. Some athletes may have three or four moves that are repeated over and over, while others have a seemingly unlimited number of moves to call upon in any given situation. Much of this is dependent upon an athlete's overall motor-control, often referred to as athleticism. Many factors go into athleticism, but most of the literature in this area suggests that the most effective way to improve this is to give the athlete as much motor control stimulation as possible in as many different ways as possible. This means allowing kids to play multiple sports, participate in a wide range of physical challenges, and spend time in environments which force a person to move the body in a variety of ways. It appears that this kind of training elicits the best results when done with young athletes under the age of 14. This is not to say that older athletes cannot benefit from general motor-control stimulation, but the developing nervous system of the younger athletes may adapt more readily to this kind of stimulation.

An athlete's proprioception, or ability to know where the body is in space, can also be developed to a certain extent, but it seems that the most useful work in this area also needs to be done before complete maturation of the nervous system, usually around age 14. After this, the development of an athlete's proprioception will be smaller, but it may still be worth the time investment.

With this said, it is very appropriate to spend time developing efficient movement patterns with younger athletes. The catch here is that many young athletes really don't enjoy this kind of work on fundamental skills without the intrigue of a game, so coaches must make the drills interesting and purposeful in an effort to maximize time and maintain attention. A young athlete who learns how to efficiently move her body in multiple directions will raise her potential for the future. This does not guarantee future success, but it can give an athlete a higher potential range of abilities if proper coaching and practice are put into place.

Many coaches will inappropriately spend too much time with older athletes working on abilities such as static balancing or balancing-type tricks. This training may or may not elicit results, but the results are typically not proportionate to the amount of time spent on these activities. It has been shown that many balance drills, especially when unstable surfaces are employed, have little transfer to real life sport movement. This is because the "righting" patterns (the nervous system activity that responds to a loss of balance and repositions the body in an effort to regain balance) used on unstable surfaces such as stability balls, balance boards, etc. are very different from the reflexive patterns used on the ground. And, because most sports are played on a surface that does not move, it does not seem prudent to spend very much time or effort on this.

This time and effort could be used to effectively improve other physical, technical or tactical skills or reinforce the righting patterns utilized on the ground (which will also be used in competition). The literature on skill development reveals that in order to improve a skill, the exact skill must be practiced in the exact environment in which it will be performed. Studies have shown that practicing skill A generally has a limited effect on skill B, especially when the two movements differ in any of the following ways:

- Speed of movement
- Movement complexity
- Joint angles
- Joint velocity
- Surface or equipment used
- Open vs. Closed Feedback Loop
- Muscles involved

It appears that differences in any of these areas will produce limited transfer from one skill to another. To simplify this, if you want to get better at something, you have to practice it. Additionally, it is important to practice a skill exactly as it will be used in real life. It is certainly appropriate to slow movements down and practice them as closed skills early in development, but eventually the skills need to be practiced at game speed and in a game-like environment if they are to be used effectively in competition.

All of this relates to the teaching progression used in this system. The idea is to begin practicing the skills at a slow pace in a closed feedback environment. When the fundamental movements are mastered, the speed of movement will be increased. Next, the complexity of movements will be increased. Finally, external stimuli will be introduced so the movements can be practiced while processing environmental information. With appropriate and purposeful practice, new (and more effective) movement patterns can be introduced into an athlete's physical repertoire. At this point, creative coaching will help athletes introduce the practiced movement patterns into game-like situations.

To begin the process, we must look at the fundamental components of agility and begin practicing them in controlled environments. Some of this may seem rudimentary, but don't assume that all athletes are doing everything correctly. In fact, assume that they are not moving correctly until they demonstrate that the fundamental components have been mastered.

Fundamentals of Agility: The 5-Fs

Most agility movements utilize five fundamental principles. These guiding principles can be remembered by understanding the 5-Fs:

Fundamental Phases of a Change of Direction

Feet

Funnel (Inverted)

Force Vectors

Forward Lean

Each fundamental has several components that impact agility performance. Together they form the foundation of agility mechanics and guide all training programs intended to improve agility performance. Of course, there are exceptions to each of these fundamentals, but when the 5-Fs are thoroughly understood and applied to movement, athletes will be better able to safely and efficiently change directions during competition.

Agility Fundamental #1

Fundamental Phases of a Change of Direction

It is crucial to understand the seven fundamental phases of a change of direction (COD) or agility movement. These terms will be used throughout this section to describe the sequences involved in multi-direction agility movements.

1. Initial Deceleration – This includes the step before foot plant as well as the early deceleration involved during foot plant.

2. Foot Plant – Refers to the motion of planting the foot that will decelerate the body and provide the new acceleration.

3. Terminal Deceleration (Eccentric Contractions) – This is the point at which the deceleration of the body comes to a complete stop before re-initiating movement in a new direction.

4. Amortization Phase – The time between eccentric contraction (deceleration) and concentric contraction (acceleration) of the muscles involved in the movement.

5. Redirection & Acceleration – This refers to the concentric contractions of the muscles involved in initiating movement in a new direction after the amortization phase.

6. Push Off – The point at which the plant foot pushes off and leaves the ground after concentric contractions of the involved musculature create movement.

7. First Step – This refers to the first step of the inside, or non-planting, foot in a new direction after the COD takes place.

Agility Fundamental #2
Feet

Outside Foot (Plant Foot)/Inside Foot (First-Step Foot) - Fig. 5.1

In any change of direction (COD), you have an inside foot and an outside foot. The outside foot is the foot used to plant, decelerate, and redirect the body in a new direction. The inside foot is closest to the direction you are about to move, and takes the first step in the new direction. Both feet play important roles in any COD and need to be used properly in order to demonstrate great agility.

The outside foot should be planted on the ground perpendicular to the direction in which you are about to move. If the foot is not planted close to perpendicular to the new direction, you will not get an optimal push-off, and redirection will be compromised. This foot is responsible for most of terminal deceleration, redirection and acceleration during the change of direction. The leg of the outside foot must slow the body down to a complete stop and reinitiate movement in a different direction. This is quite difficult for many athletes, especially at high speeds, as it requires a tremendous amount of strength

Fig. 5.1 Outside foot (on left), inside foot (on right)

and control. Temporarily, all of the weight will be placed on the outside leg while the inside foot is repositioned for movement in a different direction.

Because the demands placed on the outside foot are so high, the inside foot will help initiate deceleration before a COD. On the last step before foot plant, the inside foot can basically "tap on the brakes" so the outside leg does not have to do all of the work. It should not slow you down too much, as this will "telegraph" the COD, but the slight deceleration from this last step will really help the outside leg with terminal deceleration.

As terminal deceleration takes place, the inside foot will be un-weighted so it can be repositioned to point in the new direction you are trying to move. The outside foot must stay wide, and it is vital that it takes the first step after push-off in the *appropriate direction*. Because it is so difficult for an athlete to properly use the outside foot, it is very common to see the inside foot placed improperly in a misguided effort to make the movement easier to control. Many athletes will put the inside foot down too close to the outside foot or too far in the direction that momentum has taken it, thereby creating inefficient movement.

Improper first-step foot placement is typically responsible for an athlete using a cross-over step, or "rounding corners" directly after push off. While a cross-over step will certainly be used in some situations, it should be taught as a separate skill. The key to great agility is the ability to change direction multiple times during one play or game sequence. If a cross-over step is used for the first step, the athlete is fully committed to movement in one direction. This may be appropriate if you are sure another COD will not be needed. If another re-direction is necessary at the point where the cross-over step is used, the athlete will be required to take an additional step to get into position for the next COD. This extra step causes you to turn your back to your opponent and is all it takes for him/her to get by you and force you into a pursuit – not a great place to be.

Common Mistakes

Rounded movement, Fig. 5.2: When the first step is not taken in the new direction, it creates "rounded agility." Basically, rounded agility is a COD that creates rounded patterns. If you could watch an athlete from above and trace lines over his movement patterns, the most effective CODs would leave sharp angles. Rounded agility would create sweeping, rounded lines. Rounded agility forces you to travel a longer distance to get to your destination. It also allows an opponent extra time to reposition himself if the initial COD created some separation.

Not all CODs need to be made at 180°, or even 90°, but a sharp movement makes it more difficult for an opponent to stick with you. It is much more difficult to react to an athlete making sharp movements than it is to stay with someone using rounded agility.

Outside foot does not plant perpendicular to the new direction, Fig. 5.3: When this occurs, it makes it much more difficult for the athlete to decelerate and makes it nearly impossible to redirect movement in a new direction.

Fig. 5.2 Rounded agility. Momentum carries the inside foot forward, rounding the angle in the COD.

Fig. 5.3 Outside foot (on left) did not plant perpendicular to the new direction. This does not allow for optimal push-off.

Agility Fundamental #3
Funnel (Inverted)

Body Low & Feet Wide

Optimal execution for a COD will have the feet wide and the body low. Imagine a funnel turned upside down (inverted) where the top is thin and the bottom is wide. This is what the body should look like during a COD. Keeping the feet wide will create greater shin angles (this will be covered in more depth in Fundamental Component #3). The hips, knees, and ankles will be bent, positioning the athlete low to the ground. Lowering your center of gravity allows for greater body control during deceleration and coils the body in preparation for the acceleration phase.

It has also been shown that a knee bend (on the outside leg) of greater than 15° greatly reduces the incidence of non-contact knee injuries. This is especially important for female athletes who run a far greater risk of sustaining severe knee injuries. Interestingly, female athletes seem to make CODs with a knee bend of less than 15° far more often than males. Cutting with a relatively straight leg (less than 15° bend) allows the upper leg and hip to begin movement in a new direction while the foot stays planted on the ground. Without proper knee bend, it will be more difficult for the involved musculature to maintain the integrity of the limb and tremendous twisting can occur at the knee. The foot should rotate on the ground as the knee and hip rotate. If the knee is not bent, it makes it much more difficult for this to occur.

Improper foot gear, such as long cleats on short grass, can also contribute to this problem as they may not allow the foot to rotate when planted. Be aware of this when selecting foot gear. For more information on foot gear, see Chapter 3.

In dealings with thousands of athletes, a low body position seems far more comfortable for males than for females. This may be due to the greater relative strength found in males, but many studies show females have nearly equal lower body strength relative to body weight. Perhaps, then, males are taught to stay low differently than females. Maybe the wider hips and greater Q-angle is responsible for these movement patterns. Whatever the reason, it is important, both for performance as well as injury prevention, to teach athletes to stay low during any COD.

Standing tall during a COD also creates more stabilization work for the upper body. Often, momentum carries the upper body in the original direction of movement during a COD. It may appear as though the athlete "collapses" at the hips at terminal deceleration. This may be due to a lack of core strength, but it is often due to improper trunk positioning which will be covered in Fundamental Component #4.

Keeping the inside foot wide allows you to initiate movement in a new direction without over-committing to that direction. It gives you the option of re-directing your movement again if necessary, which is an extremely important option when dealing with opponents. Understanding this concept also gives you valuable insight as to how to out maneuver an opponent.

Knowing that many athletes are not prepared for a second directional change, it is apparent that two quick directional changes (if done properly and with good speed) can often create separation between you and a defender. The two directional changes must be timed properly in order to take advantage of the defender while he/she is in the middle of a cross-over step. Proper timing of this second move will "freeze" the defender and give you the space you need to make a play. The defender's feet will typically come together which makes it impossible to quickly initiate movement in a new direction. If you've ever been in this position (and we've all been there), you know what it feels like. It is the lower-limb equivalent of being "handcuffed" while trying to catch a ball. Hopefully, this illustration will help you recognize the importance of keeping your feet wide and taking the first step with the inside foot.

Agility Fundamental #4
Force Vectors

Create Optimal Force Vectors - Fig. 5.4

Creating positive angles to the ground is where physics can help you become a more agile athlete. Without getting into physics here (who wants to study physics anyway?) the reality of the situation is that understanding force vectors can help make a faster, more agile athlete.

Fundamental #3 explained the importance of keeping a wide base during a COD. Taking this concept one step further, in addition to keeping your feet away from your body, you must also create a positive angle between your shin and the ground. This will allow you to push into the ground at an angle which will propel you in the opposite direction. We've all heard that for every action, there is an equal and opposite reaction. This physics adage explains that if we fail to create a positive shin angle (i.e., we are standing too upright) the force applied to the ground will create more of a vertical reaction than horizontal acceleration. In agility, we are generally trying to change our direction in the horizontal plane. That is, we are trying to move side-to-side, rather than up and down. Of course vertical changes are an important part of athleticism, but for purposes of this discussion we will assume that the athlete is trying to change directions horizontally.

Fig. 5.4 The white arrow represents the approximate force vector created during this COD.

In all CODs on the ground, there is a both a horizontal and vertical component to the movement. When you push off the ground to change directions, some of the force carries you horizontally, and some of the force carries you vertically. The sum of these forces creates what is known as a force vector. A force vector is essentially an imaginary arrow that would point in the opposite direction in which you are pushing against the ground. In a biomechanics laboratory using motion analysis and high-tech force plates, scientists are able to show the force vector an athlete creates during push off; it looks like an arrow that points in the direction the athlete is traveling.

In a perfect vertical jump, for example, all of the force would carry you vertically and your force vector would point straight up. If, however, you lost your balance during the jump and traveled sideways a bit, there would now be a horizontal component, and the force vector would have a slight angle. During an optimal COD, we want the force vector to be as horizontal as possible, so as to optimize the horizontal component and create faster movement.

The sharper the angle of the shin to the ground, the greater the horizontal forces, and the more upright we stand, the greater the vertical forces will be. This does not mean, however, that we should try to get the shin parallel to the ground and create a totally horizontal force vector. The human body does not work this way, and will not allow us to assume this position. Because the ground surface, ankle mobility, body positioning, strength, and shoe surfaces all affect our ability to create these angles, it is impossible to create a completely horizontal force vector, and it is impossible to determine the exact angle that should be used to make every movement optimal.

Think about tennis for a minute. Playing tennis on a traditional court surface is very different than playing on clay or grass. Certain players seem to excel on particular surfaces, and Agility Fundamental #3 can help explain some of this. On clay, for example, an athlete can run very fast to make a shot, plant his foot and actually slide for several feet before he comes to a complete stop and can re-accelerate in a different direction. Some athletes seem to feel more comfortable in this environment than others, and they can use this to their advantage. Creating very sharp force vectors on clay will often result in the loss of footing; athletes may slip and fall if the angle is too great and the shoe surface loses traction. On a traditional synthetic surface, however, the athlete can create much sharper force vectors and take advantage of the traction this surface allows.

The same goes for football, soccer, baseball, rugby or any other sport in which the surface may change due to weather conditions or upkeep. Athletes must be able to adjust to different surfaces if they are to maintain their footing. Imagine playing basketball on a dusty floor. You may be nice and low to the ground, have your feet wide and create the perfect shin angle and force vector, only to have your foot slip out from under you because your shoe could not "grip" the floor. You often see players licking their fingers and wiping them on their shoes to improve traction. Others wipe their soles on their socks and many people now step on a tacky product called Slip Not before entering the game. Slip Not and similar products help clean your shoes and add a touch of stickiness, giving you additional traction. All of this is done so the athletes can create the optimal shin angles/force vectors without slipping. If the surface is slippery, the athlete cannot create such a steep shin angle, which will ultimately slow him down in a game.

Ankle mobility also impacts the ability to create optimal force vectors. Athletes with a history of ankle injuries often have an impaired range of motion in this area. This can have a negative impact on an athlete's ability to apply force into the ground. The athlete will have to maintain a more erect shin angle just to avoid pain.

Taking all of these variables into consideration, the optimal force vector for a COD will be somewhere between 30° - 60° from the ground. This seems like quite a wide range, but there is no perfect angle for every person and every surface. In general, athletes should attempt to create the sharpest possible angles for optimal performance. The optimal situation would be to enhance horizontal forces while limiting vertical forces to create a force vector pointing directly in the direction you want to travel.

During warm ups, it is always a good idea to experiment with the playing surface to give yourself an idea of what is possible. Perform a few direction changes with varying shin angles to see how far you can push the force vector without too much risk of slipping. Again, selecting proper foot gear can dramatically affect performance.

Agility Fundamental #5
Forward Lean

Trunk Control – Fig. 5.5

Taking the shin angle concept upward, the ability to properly control and align the upper body must also be addressed as it can have a major impact on the force vector. As stated earlier, a lack of trunk control may be the result of inadequate core strength. This needs to be addressed with an appropriate strength-training program. If improving core strength was all that needed to occur, this would be an easy one. Unfortunately, a lack of proper trunk *control*, not just strength, is often the problem.

To optimize the acceleration phase of any COD, the trunk should be leaning slightly in the new direction. The head and shoulders need to be in front of the center of gravity if the legs are to create maximum horizontal force.

Generally, there are two ways to initiate movement from a standing position. First, a false step (a step in the opposite direction you are about to travel) can be taken to create an angle in which to push into the ground. Second, the body can lean forward to create the angle. Optimally, both of these concepts will be used during a COD.

Picture yourself running forward as fast as you can. Your body will be fairly upright or leaning slightly forward. You realize that you need to suddenly change your direction 90° to the left. Your left leg will initiate deceleration before your right foot plants

Fig. 5.5 Trunk control. The upper body leans in the direction you will be traveling.

on the ground slightly to the right of your COG. Your right leg will further decelerate the body, and will re-initiate acceleration to the left. As push off occurs the trunk will lean to the left as you prepare to move in the new direction. Your left leg, in this case, will take a small step to the left, with the toes pointed toward the new destination. This is how a typical COD will occur.

Now imagine the above example, but this time your trunk does not lean to the left during push-off. As you go through the difficult push off phase, the trunk will "collapse" and almost stay in one place while the legs are trying to move in a new direction. It would sort of look like a Road Runner cartoon where the feet run away, but the upper body stays in place for a minute before it catches up. This kind of movement pattern will not allow for optimal speed during a COD and needs to be addressed through education and practice.

The trunk plays a very important role in initiating movements and maintaining optimal body positioning during CODs. It is difficult to practice some of these leaning motions at very slow speeds because the proper execution will create rather quick movement in the new direction simply by pushing the center of gravity that way. In this case, speed up the drill slightly so the athlete can actually feel the correct movement.

When maximum acceleration is not desired, there is an even greater demand for trunk control. There are many situations when agility skills are utilized, but the athlete does not try to accelerate as hard as possible. Typically this will occur when the athlete has possession of a ball, and several moves are necessary to evade a series of defenders. Maximum body control is needed, but not necessarily at maximum speed. In this case, the trunk needs to stay more upright, with the feet moving rapidly underneath, or outside of, the body. If the trunk is swaying side to side it is much more difficult to quickly move side to side.

Another example of upright trunk control is playing defense in many sports. Because the arms may be critical to correct defensive play (such as in basketball), it is important to keep the body upright so the arms can function optimally at the same time the body is positioned for multiple CODs. Coaches should be able to explain which situations require a more upright posture vs. which situations require a greater need for acceleration.

Agility Drill Progression

Putting the Five Fundamentals together gives you an understanding of the movement involved in many agility skills. Whether you are learning these skills for your own use or to coach others, it is important to understand the proper teaching progressions involved in learning these skills. Like most forms of physical training, agility drills should follow a progression from simple to complex. While this seems like an obvious concept, many coaches allow athletes to progress too quickly, even if mastery of the simple drills is not obtained. The following sequence of drills should be followed when learning COD mechanics and incorporating them into a sport:

1. Closed skills, slow speeds,
2. Closed skills, fast speeds
3. Simple open skills, slow speeds
4. Simple open skills, fast speeds
5. Complex open skills
6. Light-contact agility drills
7. Full-contact agility drills
8. Situational practice

Closed-Skill Practice
These movements allow an athlete to practice the Five Fundamentals beginning at slow speeds and working up to faster speeds in predicable environments without having to react to external stimuli. Whenever possible, movement patterns should be practiced at slow speeds before being performed at full speed. Eventually, athletic movements need to be practiced at game speed for meaningful skill development to occur, but the initial learning phase of a new movement pattern can be slowed down so the athlete has a chance to explore the movement under complete control. When the movement patterns are acceptable, the speeds should gradually be increased to game speed.

Open Skills/Reactionary Drills
Once the movements are mastered in closed-loop environments, open-loop environments can be introduced. The external stimuli should be easily recognizable at the beginning of this phase to give the athlete the opportunity to successfully apply the movement principles in an environment which requires cognitive processing. At least one other person must be involved at this point, and game-like drills can be implemented to help the athlete recognize external cues. Keep the speed and complexity as simple as possible when initiating this kind of drill.

Begin this process by including a verbal or visual cue from a coach. The coach may point in different directions as in a "Wave Drill" or call out numbers that are associated with different directions. The athlete may also be required to wait for a coach's command before commencing a drill. Any kind of reaction from a verbal or visual cue can be incorporated into a drill to bring it closer to a real life situation. The idea here is to work on perfecting movement patterns while having to react to an outside stimulus. Oftentimes, movement patterns change dramatically when an athlete's mind shifts from the movement to the stimulus.

Be patient when introducing an outside stimulus because most athletes are not accustomed to utilizing excellent movement patterns while reacting to a stimulus. They are more accustomed to changing directions at a stationary cone or line where they can concentrate only on the movement. Many athletes will rush their movement to simulate game speed, but their mechanics will fall apart. If this happens, slow the athlete down to encourage proper mechanics. Utilizing faulty mechanics at faster speeds will do nothing but reinforce the faulty movement patterns.

Begin the reaction drills with coaching cues, and progress to reacting to another athlete with less obvious cues that mimic sport-specific situations as closely as possible. Mirror drills, such as in Fig. 5.6, or the game of tag are good examples of more advanced open-loop drills, but many of the drills in this book can be adjusted to incorporate an opponent. Simply having another athlete present in a drill will force the athlete to adjust and make sudden changes of direction.

Fig. 5.6 Mirror Drill

Through practice, the goal is to have the athlete perform quick CODs with good technique. A good coach will be able to give feedback during these drills which is important because the athlete may not be completely aware of their footwork during a "live" drill. If the proper groundwork has been laid, the footwork will be fairly sound and only minor adjustments will be made. If, however, movement mechanics fall apart when an opponent is introduced to a drill, it may be necessary to slow down and spend additional time working on the movements.

Contact Agility Drills - Fig. 5.7

Once movement patterns are mastered during reaction drills with an opponent, controlled physical contact with blocking pads can be introduced. There are obvious concerns involved when including physical contact in agility drills, so safety must always be a priority. This contact is not relevant to all sports and the amount and intensity of the contact will vary from sport to sport. For example, the contact a basketball player needs to prepare for is different than the contact involved in rugby or football. An athlete involved in a completely non-contact sport, such as tennis, has no reason to include these drills in a training program.

In practice, it is important to mimic the kind of contact seen in the sport while minimizing the risk of injury. Just because a football player may get gang-tackled in a game does not mean that it is appropriate to do so

Fig. 5.7 Agility drill with contact using a blocking pad

in practice, especially during agility or movement training sessions. The contact used in these drills is included so the athlete can practice game-like footwork in a relatively safe environment. The person providing the contact must be aware of the training goals and needs to have the best interest of the athlete in mind at all times. The goal is to practice movement technique and footwork in a "live" environment, not place an unprepared athlete in a potentially dangerous situation. An adequately cushioned blocking pad should always be used for these drills and a relatively soft surface is recommended on the ground in case an athlete falls. Physical contact between athletes without a pad is a completely unnecessary risk that has no additional benefits over using a pad.

When used appropriately, including physical contact in agility drills has the potential to dramatically increase the usefulness of training and meaningful transfer to the sport. Most athletes involved in contact sports will enjoy the "live" feel of the drills, and they will be motivated to give an all-out effort. It is easy to get lazy on a drill when only one athlete is involved, but competition will usually raise the level of intensity. And when contact is introduced, most athletes will respond with 100% effort.

Physical contact can creatively be incorporated to just about any drill described in this book, but never utilize full-contact agility drills in the following situations:
- There is a large size discrepancy between athletes.
- One of the athletes is injured.
- Movement patterns are not sound.
- Immature behavior (cheap shots, etc.) is expected from the athletes.
- There is "bad blood" between some of the athletes involved in the drill.
- The sport or position does not include much or any physical contact.
- Appropriate blocking pads are not available.

Situational Practice

This is the most advanced form of movement training, and is basically sport practice with an awareness of the movement patterns being utilized. In situational practice, athletes are placed in situations in which they must recognize an opponent's positioning, movement, or play call, make a decision, and respond with appropriate movement. This type of practice develops cognitive awareness and anticipation as well as proper movement patterns and footwork. If proper movement mechanics have not been mastered in less complex drills, working on them in situational drills will probably be ineffective; the drills will still develop cognitive and anticipatory skills, but the movement-training aspect of the drill will be too difficult. The athlete must have a high level of movement competence or he/she will be thinking about the movement too much. Thinking about movement patterns in game-like situations diverts the athlete's attention from what is important and leads to poor decision making.

A skilled coach is of paramount importance in situational practice. The coach must be able to create real-life situations, give the athlete a limited number of response choices, and be able to analyze both the response choice and movement patterns. Because of the complex nature of these drills, videotaping can prove very beneficial. After practice, or between drills if available, the athlete can watch himself performing the drills while the coach provides feedback. The tape can be viewed multiple times to be sure everything is covered. Always emphasize the correct movements and responses rather than focusing only on mistakes. Keep in mind that the athlete probably wants to perform the drills correctly, and simply seeing himself on video is enough feedback for many athletes to correct technical or cognitive errors.

For athletes advanced enough to work on drills like this, it is often appropriate to review game or practice video and break down both cognitive and physical skills. A good coach will be able to pause the video in the appropriate place, talk to the athlete about the situation, give him instruction, and watch how the athlete actually responded on film. The coach should also be able to point out movement patterns on the film so the athlete gains additional awareness of his body and movement tendencies.

Using this sequential progression will optimize the potential for an athlete to fully integrate the learned movement patterns into competitive environments. Many coaches and athletes do not have the patience to work through this progression, and assume (often incorrectly) that good athletes always move efficiently. Don't rush the progression. It's not a race, and the drills in the last category are not necessarily better than the ones in the first category. What is important is selecting the right drill for each situation.

Offensive vs. Defensive Agility

Most people do not distinguish between the movements utilized on offense vs. the movements utilized on defense, but there is certainly a difference. The major difference is that, on offense, you determine the speed, direction and timing of movement. On defense, you must respond to the movement of another athlete. In many ways, defensive movement is much more difficult than offensive movement because of the reaction and response time involved. When you are able to initiate the movement in any direction you choose, at any time you choose, you clearly have the advantage over anyone trying to react to your movement.

Understanding this, different movement patterns are effective for offensive movement compared to the movement utilized on defense. The cross-over step and pivot-cut may be used in certain offensive situations and can provide a distinct advantage for the offensive player.

The Cross-Over Step - Fig. 5.8
While the cross-over step is most often used when an athlete is on offense, it can also be effectively incorporated into defensive movement. It is a misunderstood and misused movement that must be practiced if an athlete is going to properly utilize it in a competitive environment. The optimal movement pattern for

speed and body control is the utilization of the outside-foot plant, but there are certain situations when planting on the inside foot (or a cross-over step) is called for.

Especially on offense (but it is not unrealistic on defense), the cross-over step may be the most useful and efficient movement for a particular situation. There are certainly situations when the outside-foot plant is simply not possible. In these situations, what is an athlete to do? Stop? Give up? Not make a move? Absolutely not. The fundamentals of agility are meant to be used as a standard, not as a rule.

Because the cross-over step generally commits the athlete to a certain direction, it works best on offense or in defensive situations where the head and shoulders must remain facing one direction while the body travels in another (e.g. a linebacker tracking a play). It can also be useful for situations in which it is acceptable to momentarily commit to moving in one direction (e.g. a linebacker changing directions because a pass was thrown to the opposite side of the field).

Fig. 5.8 Cross-over step

The cross-over step can also be used on offense to displace a defender. For example, in basketball, the first step of a drive to the hoop can be a cross-over step that puts the defender in an undesirable position on the athlete's hip. (Basketball creates many unique movement opportunities because of the pivoting used while the athlete is not dribbling. Many cross-over movements will be made as a result of these situations.) Tennis is another sport where the cross-over may be used in an effort to move quickly while maintaining eye contact with the ball or opponent. A cross-over step will also be taken to get into position for many shots. The key to the cross-over step is in understanding that it commits your movement to one direction for at least one step. If the situation allows for this, the cross-over step is a viable option.

A proper cross-over step should utilize some of the basic principles of agility. The body should stay low with a bend in the knees, and the torso is responsible for balancing the body and leaning in the direction of the intended movement. In many cases, the cross-over step will carry the body in one direction while the upper body is facing another, as in the classic carioca drill. Besides serving as a good warm up exercise for the hips, the carioca basically teaches the athlete how to utilize a cross-over step while maintaining head and shoulder positioning. Just like most drills, if the carioca drill is performed in a lackadaisical fashion, it is worthless.

Ladder drills that utilize a cross-over step serve a similar function; they create an awareness of how to position the body during a cross-over step. Unfortunately, these drills are often overused and can teach the athlete that the cross-over step is an optimal movement pattern, which it is not in many cases. When using any kind of cross-over drill in practice, it is important that the athletes are aware of how and when this movement should be utilized. The athletes should understand that practicing these movements is primarily done in an effort to prepare them for situations in which a cross-over step cannot be avoided, not as a 'first choice' movement.

In general, the cross-over step should not even be introduced as a common movement until the fundamental principles of agility can be effectively utilized in competitive situations. At this point, efficient movement patterns have been established, and the athlete is ready for a more diverse repertoire of movements.

Pivot-Cut - Fig. 5.9 & 5.10

The pivot-cut is an extremely useful movement, but it is often used in inappropriate situations. The pivot cut is very similar to the COD patterns described earlier with one major difference. The inside-foot does not un-weight to take a step in the intended direction. Instead, it stays on the ground and pivots as the outside-foot plants, crosses over, and takes the first step in the new direction. It is kind of a cross between the cross-over step and an optimal COD.

This movement is most appropriate on offense, or when you are in a position to dictate the movement. To use it most effectively, the inside foot should help decelerate the body before the outside foot plants. If executed properly, this deceleration assistance allows the athlete to go into the COD with more speed. It is very demanding to place all of the deceleration on the outside-foot, and it is difficult to do at high speeds. The pivot-cut may allow you to decelerate more quickly, giving you an advantage over your opponent. In certain situations, the plant foot may also look like a feint, and an opponent may be thrown off by the movement.

Fig. 5.9 Right foot plant during a pivot-cut

Fig. 5.10 Right foot crossing over to take the first step after a pivot-cut

Forward-to-Backward COD - Fig. 5.11 & 5.12

Another common movement in sports is changing from forward movement to backward movement, or backpedaling. This is often accomplished with several choppy steps to slow down the forward movement before backpedaling begins. While this is a decent option for an athlete too weak to rapidly decelerate, it is certainly not the fastest technique, and may not even be the safest.

The "hip-switch" technique is a more appropriate option that will allow for quicker deceleration and greater body control. In the hip-switch, the athlete simply turns the hips sideways and plants one foot perpendicular to the direction he/she will be traveling. This plant-and-cut motion is very similar to the movement pattern used in a standard COD. Turning the hips sideways allows the gluteus to participate in the movement to a greater extent and creates the "blocking" motion with the plant foot that is so important to rapid changes of direction. The greater the angle (depending on the surface) created at the shin, the greater the stopping power.

Fig. 5.11 Forward-to-backward, right foot just about to plant

Fig. 5.12 Forward-to-backward, right foot planted, left foot about to take the first step backward

Also like a standard COD, the first backpedal step will be taken with the inside foot (the one that did not plant) once deceleration is complete. This will place a great deal of stress on the musculature of the plant leg, so lower-body strength is critical.

Just like other CODs, it is important to bend the knees and keep the lead foot out in front of the body during the hip-switch technique. With the feet pointing forward, placing the feet in front of the body during deceleration has been shown to be a dangerous position. The ACL, which is designed to limit anterior translation of the tibia, may be significantly stressed during each step as there is a strong likelihood that one of the steps will be taken with a straightened knee - an extremely dangerous position for the ACL. We know that a knee bend of greater than 15° during a COD will greatly reduce the risk of injury, so it is crucial that athletes understand the importance of dropping the center of mass just before the foot is planted in this, or any other, technique.

A properly performed hip-switch, however, puts the ACL in a more protected position because of the additional musculature that is recruited as well as the positioning of the knee during deceleration. Whereas some people claim that keeping the feet under the body with choppy steps is the safest way to decelerate for ACL tear prevention, the hip-switch technique seems like a more prudent approach. It protects the ACL, and is a much quicker technique. When speed is a consideration (and it usually is with athletes), there is no question that the hip switch will provide greater deceleration and stopping power and recruits more musculature during the initial push off.

More research needs to be done in the area of ACL tear prevention, especially for female athletes, but at this time the hip switch technique appears to be a very safe and efficient way to rapidly decelerate the body during sport movement.

Backward-to-Forward COD - Fig. 5.13

When changing to forward movement from a backpedal, there are two technique options. The first is the T-Step, and the second is to use choppy steps. When decent field conditions are present, the T-step is the quickest technique, but the choppy steps version is useful when the field is slippery.

In the T-step, the backward movement will be stopped by leaning forward and placing one foot, perpendicular to the direction of intended movement, well behind the center of mass. Similar to the plant in a standard COD, placing the foot perpendicular to the direction of the new movement allows for a "blocking" effect where more surface area is in contact with the ground and more musculature can be recruited for the movement. When possible, it is optimal to decelerate with the plant foot before initiating reacceleration with a small step on the other foot. When executed properly, the movement involved in reacceleration is very similar to a standard COD.

Fig. 5.13 Backward-to-forward T-step

The quick-feet technique is often taught by coaches who like to see athletes moving their feet at all times. These coaches believe that if the feet are constantly in motion, the athlete will be better prepared to move quickly when necessary. The small, choppy steps involved in this technique are indicative of this philosophy. In this case, the athlete will take several short, choppy steps with the feet pointing forward to decelerate and initiate movement in the new direction. The deceleration phase will typically be longer with this technique, but the athlete should be in a good position to accelerate as soon as backward movement has been stopped.

Backpedal Mechanics - Fig. 5.14 & 5. 15

A common mistake in agility training is teaching the backpedal as a movement used to cover a lot of ground. This is a mistake because, unless the athlete is jogging backward without urgency to get into position, most athletes will not backpedal longer than 10 yards (usually less) before they turn and run. In fact, the first few steps of a backpedal are the most important, and should be the focus when training this movement. A forward sprint is faster than a backpedal, so transitional movement (described in Chapter 4) should also be a priority. It should also be noted that, because of the muscular recruitment involved, backpedal work is an excellent way to help develop linear speed, agility, and body control.

In many sports, the backpedal is used in defensive situations to give the defender the opportunity to face an opponent and still move with him/her. Because the opponent typically has the advantage in this case (they are moving forward and can dictate the direction of the movement) it is vital that athletes train the ability to accelerate backwards. In most cases, backpedaling is practiced over distances much longer than any situation would require. The posture, force production, and mechanics are very different for these longer backpedal runs than for a short burst backward.

Fig. 5.14 Backpedal

Fig. 5.15 Backpedalling on treadmill

For lower intensity backpedaling or for maintaining speed, the posture is fairly upright, knee bend is slight, and the hip extension small. When accelerating with a backpedal, the knee bend is much greater, there is a greater forward lean, the center of mass is lower, and the hip extension is much more pronounced.

The greatest amount of force possible should be generated through knee extension with each step during backward acceleration, so quadriceps strength is critical. A backward body lean is used when maintaining backward speed, but the forward body lean is necessary to maintain body control and allow for hip extension and long steps. A backward lean or upright posture creates short, choppy steps that do not generate as much power. The hip extension, or long backward steps, allow the leg to "pull through" before "pushing off" during each step. Lowering the center of mass also allows for more force to be applied on each step.

Backward-to-Forward Turning

While turning from a backpedal to a forward sprint is not a movement used by all athletes, it is absolutely vital that those who perform the skill perform it with perfect technique. Defensive backs in football perform this skill more frequently than most athletes, but many athletes will perform this turn during competition. A mistake in footwork typically causes a loss of balance which often leads to a dramatic loss of speed. At the point when it is necessary to perform this movement (typcially as an opponent is passing by at full speed), even the smallest loss of speed can be a disaster. Unfortunately, most coaches never teach their athletes the proper footwork involved in the backward-to-forward turn.

To begin, the athlete will be backpedaling. Just before the turn, a "pre-turn" step will be taken. If the turn will be done to the left (counter-clockwise), the pre-turn step will be taken with the right foot. The pre-turn step is nothing more than a slight inward turn of the foot. This slight inward turn of the foot begins to turn the hips, and will allow the opposite foot to open up and step in the right direction. The right direction in most cases is the exact path that the athlete was traveling. The body must turn 180° to get into position. To assist in the initiation of the turn, the left elbow will be pulled backward behind the body as the right arm drives forward in the new direction.

As the pre-turn step is taken with the right foot, the hips must open up so the left foot can land on the ground pointing in the new direction. This is called the "first step." If the hips do not open completely and the foot does not end up pointing in precisely the right direction, movement will not occur on a straight line, and speed will be compromised. Flexibility is certainly an issue here because if the hips cannot open properly, this movement will never be performed optimally.

The first step needs to be taken in the same rhythm as the backpedal steps are being taken. Acceleration will occur after the first step is on the ground. Many athletes try to rush the first step by taking a very quick, short step. The step should be a medium sized step (not too short and not overly extended) that allows the rhythm to continue until the body is completely rotated. The right arm in this case will be driven forward at this point, with the left arm pulled backward.

As the first step is taken, the head should be purposefully turned in the new direction. The head will help dictate the direction of movement, so get the head rotated quickly. After the head turns and the first step is taken, the rest of the body should begin leaning forward to help accelerate. This forward lean should not occur until the hips turn and the first step is on the ground. If the forward lean is created too early, the body will lean in the wrong direction and balance will be compromised. After the forward lean is initiated, the back foot will begin taking the second step in the new direction. At this point, sprinting mechanics can begin as acceleration takes place.

Chapter 5 Coaching Tip

When teaching new skills, try this three-step approach:

1. Introduce, Explain & Demonstrate: Explain the importance of the skill, its role in sports, and how it may impact the athletes' performance. As you physically demonstrate the skill, verbally explain the most important aspects of the skill. Be as clear and concise as possible, focusing on *how* to perform the skill rather than how *not* to perform the skill.

2. Practice: Choose drills that appropriately allow the athletes to practice the skill. Allow for multiple repetitions of the skill so the athletes can experiment with how to perform them. When possible, give the athletes time to practice on their own so mistakes can be made without anyone watching. Then, bring them into a more structured environment where the skills can be practiced over and over again.

3. Provide Feedback & Correct Problems: Once practice has begun, the coach needs to provide constructive feedback to correct problems. Again, focus on what *to do*, not what *not to do*. Once the skill has been practiced thoroughly, the coach can begin to give more pointed feedback to correct problems. At this point, the athletes will have a decent feel for the skill and will be ready for corrective feedback.

This approach is the optimal way to help athletes learn skills. Of course, the coach always needs a solid understanding of the skill and a trained eye to notice technical errors. If these skills are in place, this three-step approach can assist the coach in developing athletic movements.

Chapter 6

Agility Drills

This section includes a variety of agility drills that can be used in almost any setting. Whether you are working by yourself, with a partner or coach, or with an entire team, with a little creativity, these drills can be incorporated into any workout. In some cases, several variations of a drill are given. There is no end to the number of variations that can be used in each drill. If you have something specific that needs work, use your creativity and modify these drills in any way that will make them more appropriate for your situation. Feel free to utilize them in any way that might help you.

For example, you can use different versions of the 4-Cone drill with just about every different sport imaginable – football, soccer, tennis, baseball, softball, lacrosse, basketball, rugby, etc. Just make sure to choose patterns that closely resemble the movement patterns of an actual game.

A lot of agility drills are used inappropriately. There is no magic to any of the agility drills; their purpose is to work on technique. Unfortunately, a lot of people use them more for anaerobic conditioning purposes than for technique work. In some cases, it is very appropriate to use agility drills for anaerobic conditioning. At the end of a workout, after technique has been worked on, some agility drills are wonderful conditioning tools. But, if the goal is to improve agility mechanics, plenty of rest should be given between sets, and an emphasis should be placed on movement patterns.

The Mirror Drill (above) is an excellent way for athletes to practice footwork skills against an opponent. While it is a great drill, it should only be used when an athlete is ready. None of the drills included in this chapter are magical, but they all offer substantial benefits when used appropriately.

2-Line Teaching Drill

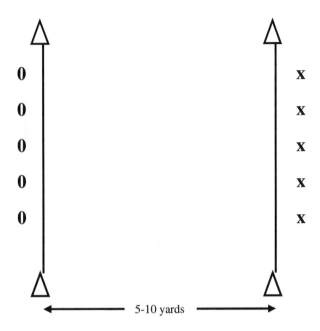

This drill is perfect for teaching change of direction mechanics, especially during the first few sessions with an athlete, or with a group of athletes working on foundational movement training. A creative mind can come up with an endless number of variations on this basic drill.

Create two rows of athletes, 5-10 yards apart, facing each other. In the figure, the O's will simply run to the opposite line, make a cut, and return to their original position. When the O's are done, the X's will go. You can do multiple repetitions of the same movement, or give directions each time and create a new variation for each repetition.

This is a good teaching drill because the coach can stand between the two lines to demonstrate and give directions. Because it is a very simple drill, the athletes can concentrate on their movement patterns. Initially, it can also be done at relatively slow speeds, and the speed can increase as the athletes begin to master the movement patterns.

Variations include:

Sprint – Sprint	Start from push up position
Sprint – Backpedal	Start laying on back
Sprint – Shuffle	Perform drill 3 times in a row
Shuffle – Sprint	Butt spin between lines
Shuffle – Shuffle	Squat-thrust at each line
Forward roll each way	Use your imagination

Basic Angle Cutting Drills

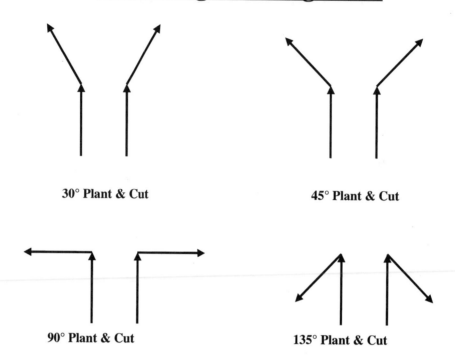

30° Plant & Cut

45° Plant & Cut

90° Plant & Cut

135° Plant & Cut

These drills can be used as basic skill training, for rehabilitation, or for advanced training depending on the speed, reactive requirements, and condition of the athlete. They are perfect for training basic change of direction mechanics and can be incorporated into a variety of situations.

As long as proper mechanics are utilized, these simple drills can help an athlete develop or reinforce neural pathways. Balls, opponents, and physical contact can be incorporated to create more realistic situations. A coach can also call out the pattern on the fly to enhance the "reaction" aspect of the drill.

Zig Zags

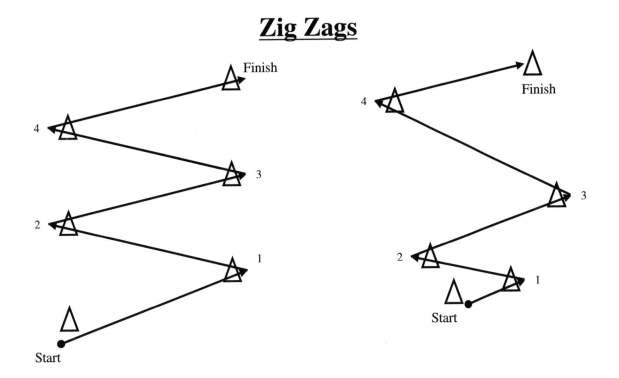

Zig-Zags are used to work on the basic mechanics involved in a change of direction. The cones can be set up with even spacing or in a varied pattern depending on the goals of the athlete. Fairly realistic cutting angles can be achieved by moving the cones in different positions.

Rather than bringing both feet around each cone, as many coaches suggest, more realistic movement mechanics can be used if only the outside foot is required to go around the cone. The inside foot can then stay relatively wide and initiate movement in the new direction without having to "swing" around the cone, which is not a realistic movement pattern and should not be practiced. Because the cones will end up between the feet, it is best to use short cones (under 12"), agility rings, or disks.

This is a great drill to use when teaching mechanics. The realistic angles involved also make it an excellent foundational drill for advanced athletes.

4 Corners

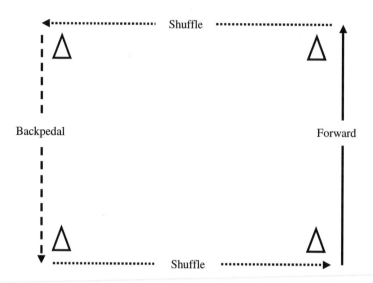

The movements can be changed depending on the needs of the athlete. The most important aspects to work on are performing clean transitions between movements and sharp cuts at each corner.

Create competition by placing one athlete at each corner. Start everyone at the same time, and the drill ends when an athlete catches the one in front of him/her. This can be an excellent drill to work on COD mechanics as well as adding a conditioning component in a competitive environment.

For rehabilitation purposes, this drill can be used to very slowly reinitiate the athlete to planting on one foot. You may choose to simply jog around the cones, planting on the outside foot at each corner to help the athlete gain confidence in the injured area. This is very important in ACL rehabilitation. Once an athlete is cleared for this type of movement, many are very tentative and need a great deal of work to relearn efficient movement patterns. Without specific work to reestablish proper movement, a comeback from this type of surgery will be incomplete. Basic drills such as this one are perfect to slowly integrate agility training into the rehabilitation process.

3-Cone Movement Change Drill

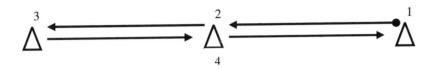

This simple pattern can give life to an endless number of variations. Think about the movements involved in your sport, and create a drill that mimics them. Athletes love variation, so get creative and make this simple drill as fun as possible.

- a. Shuffle, Sprint, Shuffle, Sprint
- b. Sprint, Shuffle, Sprint, Shuffle
- c. Cross-over run, Sprint, Cross-over run, Sprint
- d. Backpedal, Sprint, Backpedal, Sprint
- e. Backpedal, Shuffle, Backpedal, Shuffle
- f. Forward roll, Sprint, Forward roll, Sprint
- g. Butt-spin, Sprint, Butt-spin, Sprint
- h. Shuffle, Butt-spin, Shuffle, Butt-spin
- i. Carioca, Sprint, Carioca, Sprint
- j. Jump, Sprint, Jump-stop, Sprint, Jump-stop, pivot 180°, repeat back to start
- k. Perform a 360° jump or turn at each cone
- l. Dribble a basketball or soccer ball through different patterns
- m. Carry a football, rugby ball, lacrosse stick, or racquet through the drills
- n. Throw or hit a ball at the athlete during the drill. Make them catch, throw, or hit while moving.
- o. Use your imagination to come up with your own ideas!

X Drill &
Other "Letter" Drills

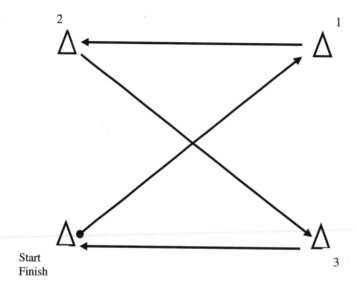

The basic "X" pattern can be used in several different ways, using various movements to traverse from cone to cone. Your imagination will allow for multiple variations.

"Letter" drills are simple cone drills that take the shape of different letters of the alphabet. Imagine a "Z-Drill" or a "C-Drill" or even a "D-Drill." Obviously, some letters lend themselves better to this drill than others, but the point is that each letter has the potential to replicate a different sport movement. D or C-Drills can be used to replicate a "curl" motion in basketball, or the rushing motion of a defensive end, or a pursuit pattern of a soccer player chasing an opponent. You'll never be at a loss for new drills as long as you can remember your A-B-C's.

3-Cone Variations

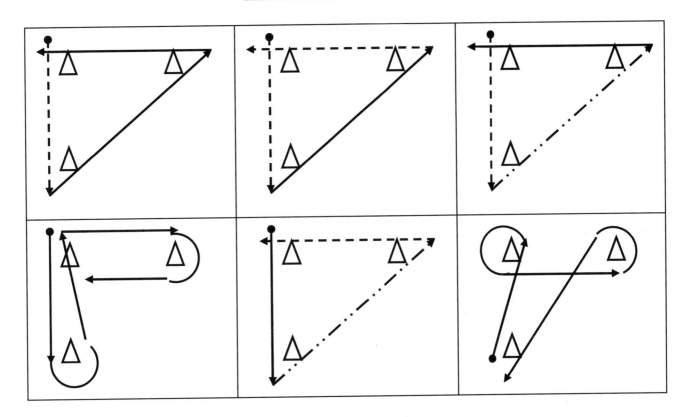

4-Cone Variations

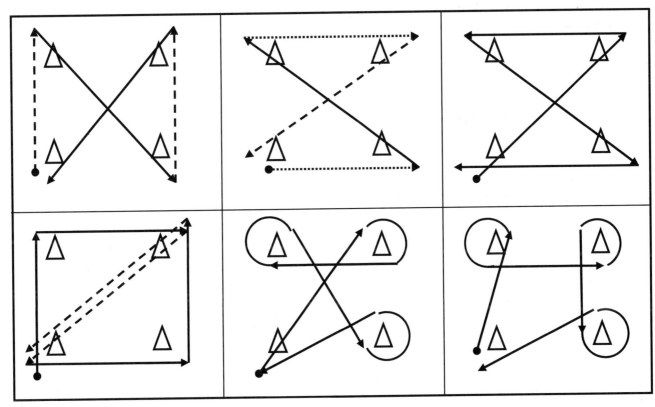

More Cone Drills

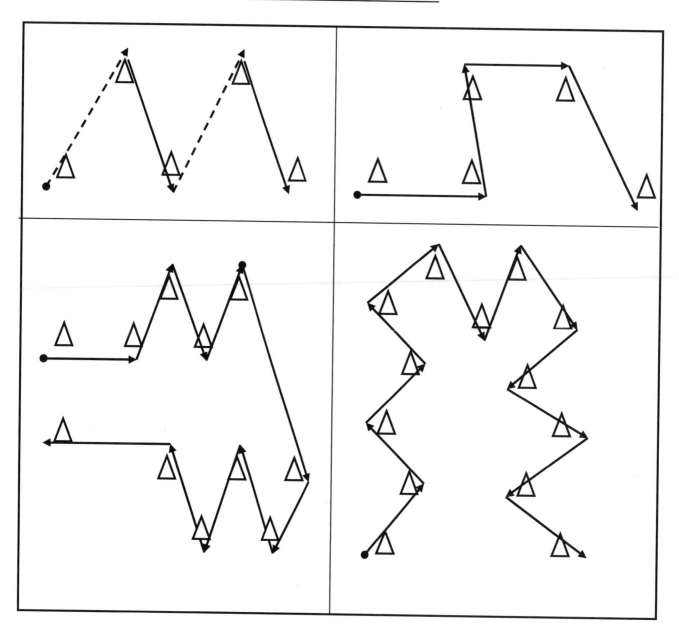

The possibilities are endless with cone drills. Try connecting two or more drills together to include a more complex drill with a transition between the two. Obstacle courses are also an excellent way to train both agility and anaerobic fitness, and many athletes love the challenge and change of pace different courses present. Use your imagination and take advantage of the opportunity to help your athletes perfect efficient movement skills.

Diamond Drill

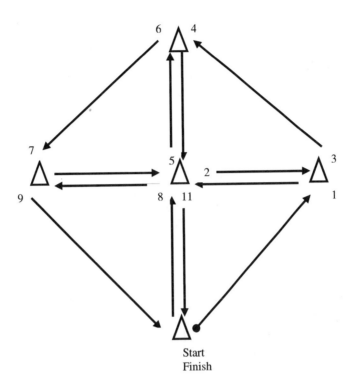

Start
Finish

This drill is set up to perform the same pattern four times per repetition. For example, you can shuffle to #1, sprint to #2, and backpedal to #3. The same pattern would then be performed to 4, 5 & 6, then 7, 8 & 9, etc. Perform the drill in the opposite direction to train the movements in both directions. You can change the movement pattern on each side of the diamond as long as the athletes are advanced enough to perform the complex patterns with proper technique and intensity.

This drill works well with small groups. Create a line at the start, and the next person in line begins when the person ahead of him/her gets to #3. This way four people can perform the drill at the same time without interrupting each other's movement.

An endless number of variations can be used in this pattern including:
- Shuffle to #1, Sprint to #2, Backpedal to #3
- Sprint to #1, Shuffle to #2, Sprint to #3
- Carioca to #1, Cross-over run to #2, Sprint to #3

The basic pattern can also be changed using the same diamond set up. For example, you can start from the middle, run to one cone and back to the middle. Then, run to another cone and back to the middle. This is a good pattern for working on jump-stops and pivots for basketball. For example, run to one cone, jump-stop, leave one foot on the ground, drop step, and shuffle back to the middle. Repeat on all four sides.

The Wheel

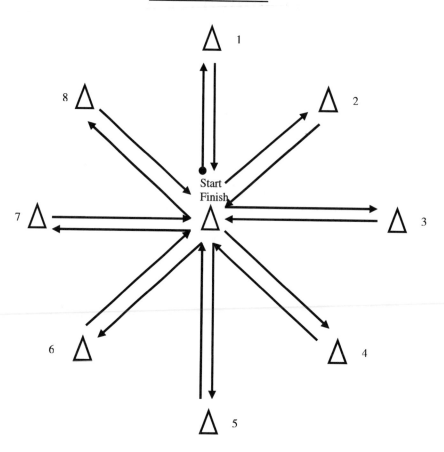

The basic pattern of this drill is outlined in the illustration, but the movements can be varied in infinite patterns depending upon the imagination of the coach. The key here is the repetitive technique work. Examples include:

> Sprint out – Sprint in
> Backpedal out – Go around partner – Sprint in
> Shuffle out – Shuffle in
> Sprint out – Shuffle in
> Sprint out – Crawl under partners legs – Leap frog partner – Sprint in
> Sprint out – Perform 3 squat thrusts – Sprint in
> Sprint out – Jump-stop – Pivot, pivot, pivot, drop step – Shuffle in
> Use your imagination to create sport-specific movements at each cone or partner.

This is a great drill to use for groups. Divide the group into two equal groups (group 1 and group 2 for this example). Each person in group 1 stands at one of the outside cones (the cones do not need to be used in a group situation), facing the inside of the wheel. Group 2 forms a small circle around the center cone, facing outward. Each person on the inside should be facing a "partner" on the outside. When the coach says GO, everyone in group 2 performs the drill, while group 1 acts as the "cones." After group 2 goes all the way around the wheel, the groups switch sides.

Zing Tao

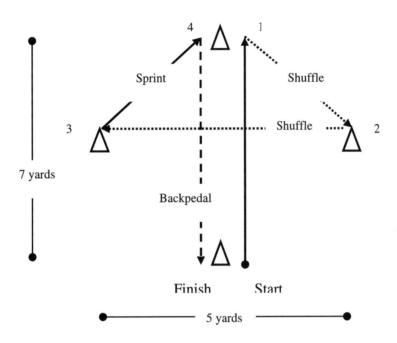

This drill is best used with at least four athletes. When the first person reaches #1, the next person in line starts. Because of the criss-crossing nature of the drill, it is important to be aware of where everyone is.

Zing-Tao also helps athletes understand how important it is to execute drills and carry out directions with precision. If the next person in line doesn't start on time, or if you cross-over to the wrong side of the cones while backpedaling, everyone is required to adjust. This is a good opportunity for a coach to discuss precision and the importance of teamwork.

When several repetitions have been performed starting from the right of the first cone, switch to the left of the first cone, and reverse the pattern.

The name Zing-Tao does not mean anything. Western Michigan University Strength & Conditioning Coach, Bob Vezeau, came up with it as a joke, and it stuck.

JK Lane Drill

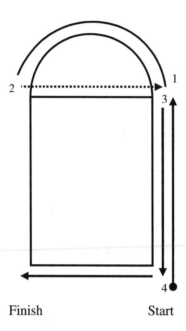

Finish   Start

Using a basketball lane (you can also create this pattern on a field using cones), start at the baseline in any position you choose. Creativity can be used here. Start from a push-up position, laying on your back, facing backward, etc. Run to the elbow (#1), and around the top of the key as quickly as possible. At #2, plant the outside foot and shuffle across the free-throw line to #3. At #3, plant the outside foot, and sprint back to the baseline. Plant the outside foot and sprint to the finish.

Instead of finishing there, you can plant your outside foot again, turn 90°, and start the drill from the opposite side of the lane.

If maximal energy is used, going around one time in each direction will be fairly taxing, but not overly demanding for most athletes. You can create a greater anaerobic demand by performing several repetitions in a row before resting.

You can also get creative and use a ball in this drill. If a partner is present, he/she can pass the ball as you shuffle across the lane. Upon receiving the pass, you can either take a jump shot, dribble, and perform a lay-up, or dribble and perform a slam dunk. The coach can keep the athlete in the drill until a certain number of shots are made.

You may also want to position players at different points in the drill to mimic a screen/pick. The athlete performing the drill can use some imagination to practice coming off a screen.

Over 2, Back 1

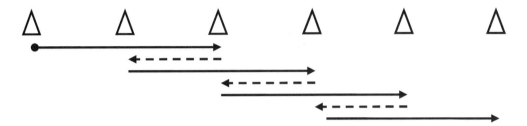

An unlimited number of variations can be used in this drill to practice sport specific movements. It can be used as a conditioning drill or to practice change of direction mechanics. Multiple lines can be formed so the drill can be used in a team training situation.

To perform the drill, place cones on a straight line about five yards apart. Run two cones forward, plant the foot, then run one cone back. Continue this pattern until you have reached the end of the line. The longer the line, the more demanding this drill will be for anaerobic conditioning. The rest periods can also be easily modified depending on the training goals.

Variations include:
1. Run forward two, backpedal one
2. Sprint two, cut, sprint one
3. Sprint two, shuffle one
4. Shuffle two, sprint one
5. Shuffle two, backpedal one
6. Carioca two, sprint one
7. Perform a push-up at each change of direction
8. Sprint two, butt-spin one
9. Sprint two, somersault one
10. Sprint one, drop-step, shuffle one
11. Add a ball to include sport skill work

Shuffle – Sprint
Transition Drill

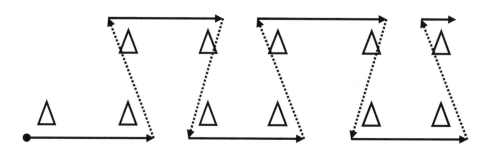

An excellent way to work on transition acceleration, this drill combines shuffling and forward sprinting. Sprint forward one cone. Go around the cone, then shuffle across and behind the next cone. Plant with the outside foot to create a sharp change of direction, and sprint forward again. The shuffle can be replaced with backpedalling, carioca, jogging, or forward sprinting. Footwork is crucial here to ensure that athletes are learning and reinforcing the appropriate neural pathways.

If this drill is used with a team, the next athlete in line will begin the drill when the person in front of him/her reaches the third (or fourth depending on the number of athletes) cone. Once an athlete has finished the drill, they should jog to the back of the line. Add a simple zig-zag drill on the return to enhance the functionality and demands of the exercise.

Pro Agility Shuttle

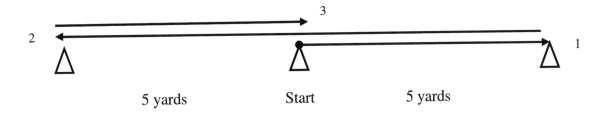

Start facing the middle cone, with your feet pointing forward, straddling the (imaginary or real) line even with the cone. Position yourself in a 3-point stance with the hand on the ground becoming the direction you will start, i.e. if the left hand is down, you will start running to the left, if the right hand is down, you will start running to the right. Some coaches use the opposite hand, so make sure you know what is expected if you are getting tested. You get to determine which way you start, but it is a good idea to practice both directions. Run to #1, and use a pivot-cut to turn 180° toward #2. Run to #2, use a pivot-cut again to turn 180°, and run through #3 like it is a finish line.

There are two ways to teach the start. The most comfortable for many athletes is to start with a cross-over step (not a very good idea in real life, but this drill is one of the most common tests of agility so it must be mastered), which allows you to get to the first cone in four steps and plant with the outside foot. This technique will utilize a pivot-cut, so make sure the outside foot plants ahead of the inside foot. This will allow the outside foot to push off and come through for the first step without having to circle around in an effort to avoid tripping over the inside foot. This works very nicely, and it a very effective way to start.

You can also start by pushing off the outside foot, and taking a small step in the intended direction with the inside foot (a real-life technique). Unlike the cross-over step, you can enlist the help of the outside arm here by swinging it forcefully in the direction you start as you take your first step. The only problem with using this technique is that you are required to get to the first cone in just three steps, or utilize a hop to get there. With practice, this is probably the fastest technique, but it is awkward for many athletes and can be challenging to teach properly. Whichever start you use, lean the head and shoulders forcefully in the direction you are traveling to help initiate the movement.

During the 10-yard sprint from #1 to #2, utilize good sprinting mechanics, taking long steps (the fewer the better for most people). Many athletes will take 5 steps, plus a hop-step to travel this distance and put themselves into position to perform another pivot-cut. Be sure to sprint hard through the finish line to get the best time possible.

3-Cone L-Drill

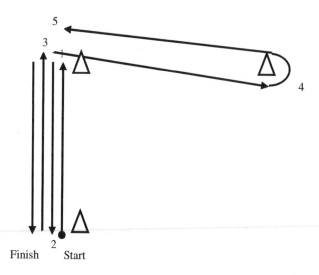

Start from the left of the first cone in a 3-point start. The pattern begins by running forward five yards and touching the ground with the right hand (plant with the right foot so you will be facing away from the cone), even with the 2nd cone. Turn 180°, run back to the starting line and touch the ground with the right hand again. Turn 180° once again, sprint forward five yards, go around the 2nd cone, and turn right. Sprint toward the inside of the 3rd cone where you will loop around it (touching the ground as you loop around the cone is not permissible) and head back toward the 2nd cone. Turn left around the second cone, and sprint back to the starting line to finish the drill.

Because it is generally required to start from a 3-point stance and touch the ground at #1 with the right hand, it is recommended to start with the right foot forward in the starting position. Many athletes are accustomed to starting with the left foot forward, but it is somewhat awkward for many athletes to touch the first line with the right hand because it is difficult to get there in three comfortable steps. By starting with the right foot forward, four comfortable steps can be taken which will position you perfectly to plant the right foot and touch the ground with the right hand.

Use a pivot-cut at #1, so that on the way back to #2, the first step will be taken with the right foot. This will allow you to take three steps to get to #2 and plant with the right foot and right hand. At #3, it is optimal to plant with the left foot when cutting to the right, but the steps do not always work out perfectly for everyone. When looping around the third cone (#4 on diagram), it is optimal to plant the left foot directly below the cone (on the diagram). Then plant the right foot above and to the right of the cone so the left foot can get around the cone and take a step in the new direction.

Football linemen are typically tested on this drill at combines, but because of the various movements involved, it is a good drill for many athletes to practice different movements.

<u>Ladder Drills</u>

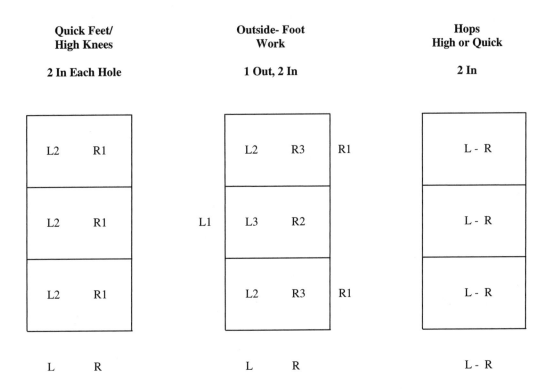

Agility ladders are often promoted as quality agility training tools, but their use for game-like movements is drastically overrated. Because the patterns are predetermined and unrealistic, they are classified as "closed skills" and should be treated as very general movement training. Their ability to enhance sport-specific movement patterns is questionable, but they are an excellent way to challenge overall motor control and coordination. Proper coaching will dramatically enhance the effectiveness of the ladder, so be sure to give plenty of instruction and feedback when they are used.

Ladder training is an excellent warm-up option and can be effectively utilized to improve overall body awareness and control. The more complex drills also have the potential to enhance overall athleticism because the athletes may improve body control.

Like other drills, the drills included here are only the beginning. An endless number of drills and variations can be created with the ladder.

Ladder Drills

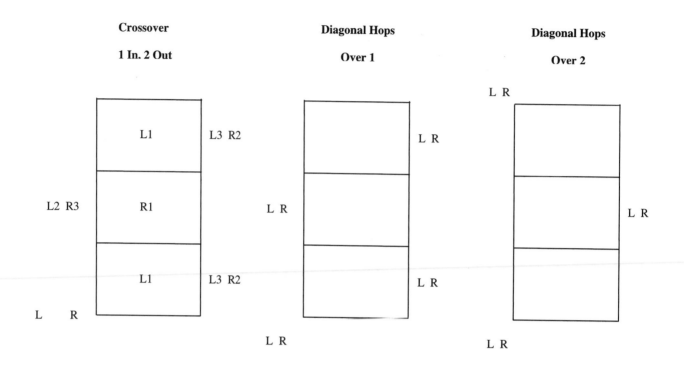

Again, these drills are simply examples of how to utilize the agility ladder. As you can see, the crossover is practiced in one of the patterns above. While the crossover step is rarely recommended in most competitive situations, it will inevitibly be used at some point. This drill will help the athlete develop the body and hip control to complete the movement without losing balance.

The hopping and jumping patterns are basically plyometic drills performed with the ladder. Variations of these patterns are easy to come up with when using the ladder because there are so many options. Jump in every hole, every other hole or every third hole. Twist or perform different movements in the air before landing each jump. You can pretend to take a jump shot or head-ball and still land perfectly in the correct hole.

<u>Ladder Drills</u>

Quick Feet

2 In. 2 Out

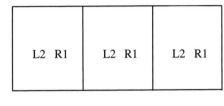

Cha-Cha
Hip Movement

1 In, 2 Out

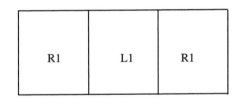

Forward &
Backward

2 In, 1 Out

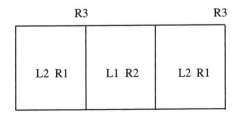

Football Receiver Routes

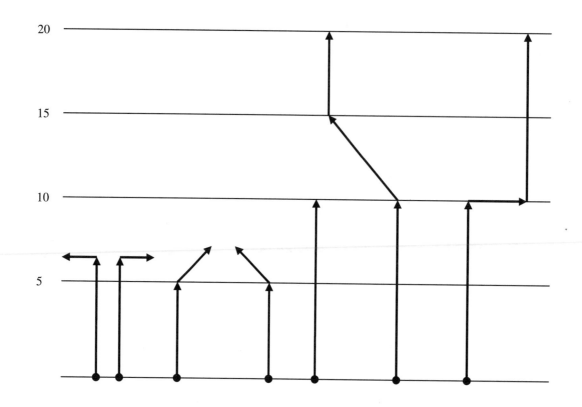

Nothing is more sport-specific than practicing the exact patterns you will be performing in competition. Most athletes do not have the luxury of knowing the specific movement patterns they will utilize in a game, but football receivers should take full advantage of this by perfecting their routes through repetitive patterns. Many receivers in the NFL have achieved success simply by running their routes with absolute precision. Since the receiver is largely able to dictate the movement (not to mention the QB is expecting them to perform the routes with precision), it would be foolish not to perfect the patterns.

Many football coaches have a running pattern "tree" that will include the routes utilized in a game. Get those patterns and practice them. The patterns listed above are simply examples if you do not know the specific routes that will be run in game situations.

Obviously, additional "reaction" agility drills need to be incorporated into a receiver's training program so that efficient movement is used even in unexpected situations.

Tight Ends can also utilize these drills in their training.

Football Running Back Drills

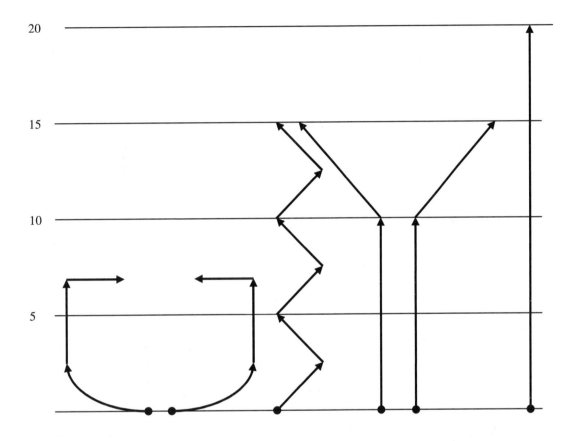

Like receivers, running backs are often called upon to run predetermined patterns. Again, these patterns should be practiced until perfected. Obviously, RBs are also required to react to different situations, so simply working on predetermined patterns will not prepare them for all situations.

Tight Ends may also benefit from these drills.

Football Defensive Lineman Drills

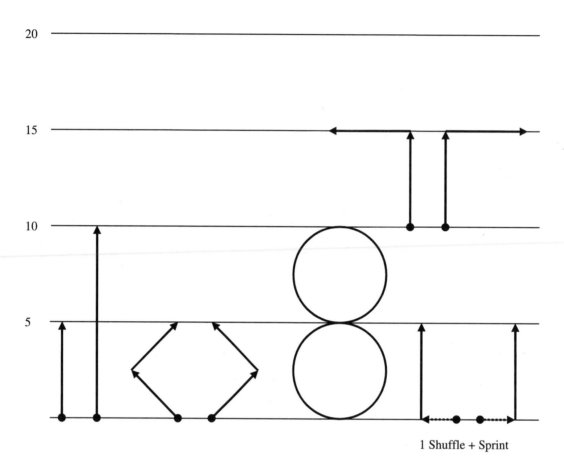

1 Shuffle + Sprint

Defensive linemen should focus on short, intense movement patterns that incorporate their position-specific skills. As often as possible, linemen should perform drills against an opponent or dummy so these skills can be mastered.

Football Offensive Lineman Drills

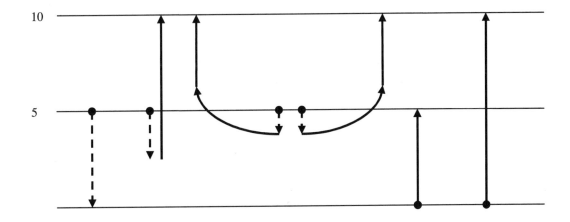

Precision is an absolute necessity for success at the position of offensive lineman. These drills mimic some of the movements used by linemen, but each coach will have specific ways in which he wants his athletes to execute drills. Take advantage of the opportunity to practice these movements when performing agility drills.

Effective hand skills and footwork are also imperative for success, so incorporating these skills into agility work is an absolute must. Incorporate contact drills as often as possible to give the athletes additional skill practice during these drills. Use pads or real opponents to simulate game-like situations.

Tight Ends can also incorporate these drills into their training.

Football Defensive Back Drills

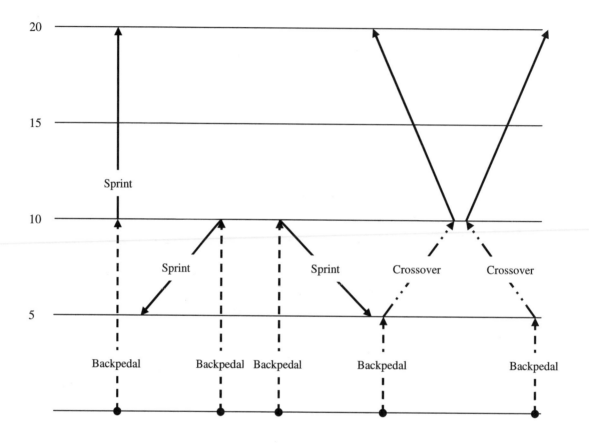

These drills will give DBs sport-specific conditioning work, and can be varied to create additional game-like situations. Because success at this position requires anticipation, recognition, reaction and appropriate responses, it is important to give DBs the opportunity to perform coverage drills against a "live" opponent as often as possible.

Watching game film and having a coach breakdown the opposition will also drastically contribute to the success of a DB. A relatively slow DB can contain an opponent if he can anticipate the opponent's movement. Coaches should teach the athlete exactly what to look for, and give him direction on how to react appropriately to different situations so the DB has the best opportunity possible to be in the optimal position to make a play.

Football Linebacker Drills

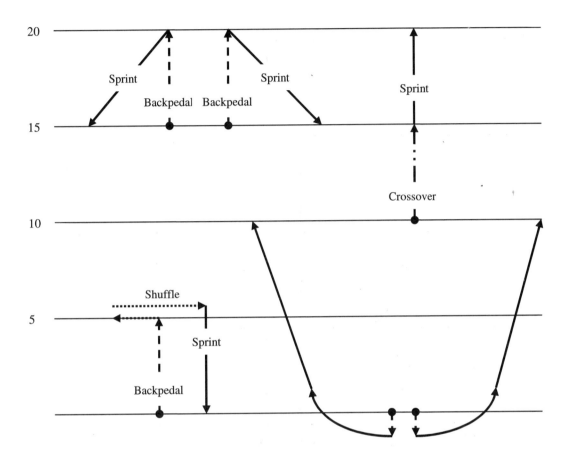

This position requires a tremendous amount of recognition and reaction to the opposition, so these specific skills need to be practiced as much as possible. The above drills should be performed in an effort to train the movement patterns involved in response to a play, but early recognition of a play is the best way to be in position to make a play. The linebacker who is in position to make a play before the physical response is necessary will appear incredibly fast and agile. The athlete who is out of position, no matter how fast he actually is, will always appear to be slow footed and will be less likely to make plays.

With this in mind, it is of paramount importance for linebackers to fully understand their opponent's tendencies. Watching game film and fully absorbing scouting reports will give a linebacker the best possible chance to succeed.

Once the above drills are mastered without having to read an opponent, the athlete should be put into situations in which he is required to utilize recognition skills and make appropriate situational responses. This is high-level agility work, and proper movement techniques should be mastered before they are used.

Football Quarterback Drills

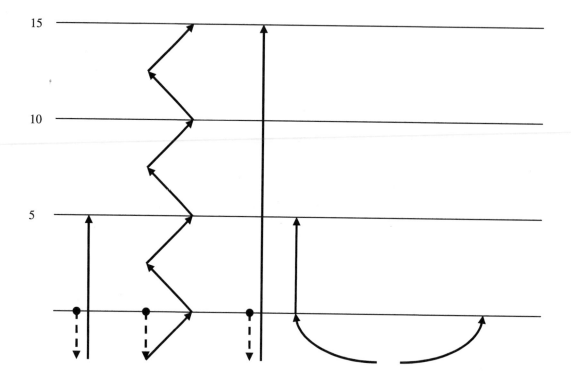

Obviously, reading the play and throwing skills are vital to quarterbacking success, but these drills can help a QB practice running movements. Bag step-over drills can also be used for QB's in an effort to enhance footwork.

Throwing to live receivers is also an absolute must for proper timing and recognition skills. Like most positions, there are numerous quarterback-specific training drills that need to be done with a qualified coach to enhance performance. These drills are beyond the scope of this book, and should be utilized for optimal QB performance.

Reaction Drills

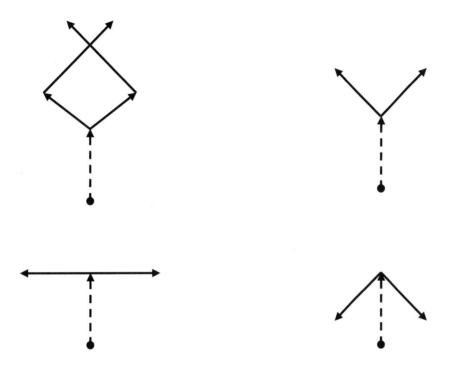

These drills train movements while incorporating reaction skills. The athlete begins the drill by backpedaling away from a coach or training partner. The coach then signals which pattern the athlete should engage in, and the athlete attempts to respond by performing the required movement. The coach can use verbal cues or hand signals for the athlete. The patterns can be varied to train specific movements.

Add a ball to make these drills even more realistic. As the athlete backpedals, the coach can throw, hit, or kick a ball in different directions to force a specific response. This drill can progress to very realistic patterns that include very specific reactions and responses.

Progress to these drills only after proper movement mechanics have been mastered. Utilizing them before proper mechanics have been developed will only reinforce faulty movement patterns, so don't rush the progression in an effort to enhance performance.

4-Corner Reaction Drill

1   2

Start

3   4

Coach stands here

The athlete begins in the center performing a foot-fire drill (running motion performed as quickly as possible). The coach can call out a number or point to a cone. The athlete then responds by running to the appropriate cone and returning to the center. Different movements can be used such as shuffling, backpedaling, cross-over runs, etc.

Enhance the difficulty by calling out multiple numbers. The athlete must run to the cones in the appropriate sequence as the coach calls out the numbers. If multiple athletes are present, they can stand at each cone. As the athlete runs toward each team-mate, a sport-specific task can be performed such as a block, jump, setting a screen, tackling (a dummy or pad is probably a better option than a human to reduce the likelihood of injury), etc.

A ball can also be incorporated for more advanced work. For example, throw, kick, or hit a ball in the direction of a cone and make the athlete react to this. The coach could also call out a situation in which the athlete must respond with an appropriate reaction.

You can also have the athlete begin the drill by facing away from the coach. On command the athlete will turn around and react to a thrown ball or any other cue you wish to incorporate. Because of the flexibility of this drill, it can be as basic or advanced as you choose.

Center Circle Drill

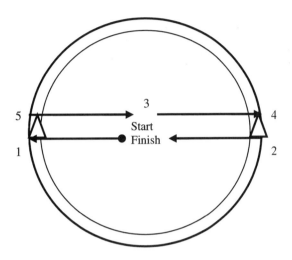

Place a cone at the "east & west" sides of a circle as shown. Begin this drill in the center of a circle (basketball courts, lacrosse fields, and hockey rinks typically have circles like this) in a ready position. Run to the outside of the circle, make a cut around one cone, and follow the "bottom" of the circle halfway around to the other cone. At this cone, make another cut and run back to the center of the circle. At the center, turn 180°, and go back the way you just came from. When this pattern has been completed twice, repeat it at the "top" of the circle.

Variations include adding a partner to "set screens" or provide contact. This makes the drill much more lifelike because of the open-skill nature of avoiding an opponent. Have the partner or coach move to various points around the circle where the athlete must make a move to avoid him/her. The partner can also hold a blocking pad and "hit" the athlete as he/she maneuvers through the drill.

Full Contact T-Shuttle

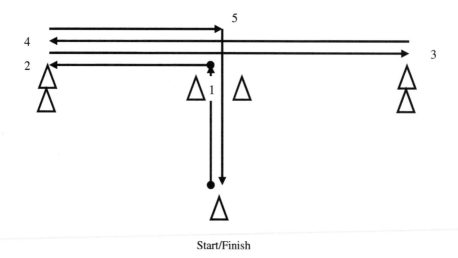

Start/Finish

This drill requires three athletes. The "offensive" athlete begins at the starting positions, and two "defensive" athletes with blocking pads stand approximately where #5 is marked on the diagram. The offensive athlete runs forward between the first two cones (the gate) and turns in either direction. He/she must run to one side, pick up one of the cones and take it to the opposite side. Put that cone down, and pick up another cone. Run it to the opposite side, put it down, and run back through the gate to the finish line.

While this drill is fairly simple, the two defensive athletes with blocking pads are "hitting" the offensive athlete as he/she tries to complete the task of moving the cones. Be sure to coach the athletes as to how much contact is appropriate for your situation so the rules are clear. Generally, no undercutting should be allowed and the offensive athlete should try to avoid contact rather than initiate it. It is also a good idea to group athletes of similar size to avoid excessive size differences.

Set boundaries for the offensive athlete so he/she must stay inside a limited space while performing the drill. The defensive athletes are only allowed on the "top" of the gate.

When the offensive athlete finishes the drill, he/she rotates to one of the defensive positions, and one of the defensive athletes goes to the end of the offensive line. So, each athlete will take one rep on offense and two reps on defense before getting a break at the end of the line.

More Drills

Mirror Drill - Two athletes face each other; one is the offensive player, the other is the defensive player. The offensive player moves side to side as if he is trying to create separation, or "get open." The defensive player simply tries to stick with him. This drill is similar to an "inbound" play in basketball or soccer, and is an excellent way to practice open-loop movements. Keep the movement along a line, rather than allowing the offensive athlete to move in all directions. Perform the drill for 5-20 seconds, then switch the athletes' roles.

Shielding Drill - Similar to the mirror drill, two players work against each other and react to each other's movements, but the Shielding Drill includes physical contact. Place a ball (or any object) on the ground with both athletes facing it, one behind the other. The front athlete attempts to "shield" the ball from the other by keeping him on his back. The athlete in the back tries to push through, or get around, the shielding athlete until he touches the ball. Both athletes must face the ball throughout the drill forcing the front athlete to use his back to shield the ball. The shielding athlete can stretch his arms out, but holding is not allowed. This is very similar to a basketball or soccer player shielding the ball, but there is a bit more contact allowed than in the actual sport.

Post-Up Drill - Position two athletes as if "posting up" in basketball. Both athletes face the same direction, with one athlete pushing his chest against the back of the other athlete. Arms and hands cannot be used in this drill. The offensive athlete will use his back and hips to move the defensive athlete backward. The defensive athlete will use his chest to push against the back of the offensive athlete in an attempt to maintain his ground. Continue the drill for a pre-determined amount of time or until the offensive player moves the defensive player a certain distance.

Sumo-Wrestling Drill - One of the most aggresive contact drills, this is only appropriate for certain sports and with experienced athletes. Begin with two athletes "locking up." This position will have each athlete's right shoulder pressed against the others chest with the head pushed against the opponent's shoulder. The right hand will reach forward to hold under the opponent's arm pit. The left hand will grip the back of the opponent's upper arm. From this position, the athletes attempt to push each other out of a pre-determined boundary. A circular boundary is best, but the coach can use whatever space is available. This drill has the potential to get somewhat violent if it is not closely monitored, so emphasize safety and closely supervise the athletes at all times.

Chapter 6 Coaching Tip

Encourage athletes to feel comfortable making mistakes so that technique can be addressed and skills can improve. Many athletes are very self-conscious and so worried about making a mistake that they don't fully invest themselves in the drill. Rather than really trying to learn a new skill or movement pattern, many athletes will simply try to get through the drill. These athletes are typically not very open to constructive feedback because it draws attention to a mistake. If athletes are this worried about making mistakes, progress will be slower than necessary.

When you sense this dynamic is present during a practice or training session (athletes will not be applying the coaching cues you are giving), it is a good idea to take a short break to explain the importance of learning the new skill and that it is 100% acceptable (even expected!) to make mistakes as long as the athletes are trying. Especially with athletes you believe are self-conscious, help them understand that nobody is judging them; the other athletes are concentrating on themselves, and the coach is there to help. Explain that corrective feedback is not meant to embarrass or draw attention to an athlete. Instead, it is given to help that athlete more fully realize his/her potential.

Of course, when athletes are learning a new skill, it is very important to give feedback constructively, making sure not to embarrass anyone or appear negative. Learning something new often brings out a feeling of vulnerability because the athletes are (temporarily) not very good at the new skill. The coach must be cognizant of this, and deal with egos appropriately so the new skill can be mastered as quickly as possible. Shattering an ego at this point will simply make it more difficult for the athlete to make progress and may impede future progress because of the increased anxiety this can create.

Chapter 7

Plyometrics

Plyometric drills take advantage of the stretch-shortening cycle of movement, which involves a rapid eccentric (negative) contraction, immediately followed by a concentric (positive) contraction. Many athletic movements (running, skipping, cutting, etc.) also take advantage of this phenomenon, so it is somewhat difficult to distinguish between what is plyometric training and what is not. Attempting to pigeonhole drills into specific categories is a waste of time. It is important to understand the purpose of drills; but rather than trying to accurately define terms and categorize exercises, the focus of this section will be on how to take advantage of different drills and methods.

Because most agility drills utilize nervous system recruitment patterns similar to plyometrics, a good agility session can elicit results similar to a plyo workout. The main differences are that agility drills can more closely simulate actual sport movement than most plyometric exercises, and agility drills generally have less jumping and landing and more of a horizontal component. In comparison to agility drills, plyos are considered "general" training. But, in comparison to strength training, plyos would be considered very "specific" training and may help you feel more explosive in a variety of situations.

There is a great deal of scientific evidence showing that plyometrics may be the link between strength training and improved speed or agility. Of course, we always need to remember that practicing proper mechanics and sport-specific movements is of paramount importance, but plyos may help your body utilize the strength you gain in the weight room when you're performing athletic movements. In an effort to enhance sport-specific movement sequences, choose plyometric drills that resemble the sport movements as closely as possible. Many coaches believe that simply practicing sport skills will help integrate increased strength (through strength training) into sport movement, and this may be true. However, a good plyometric program should augment your movement training, and help the body take full advantage of whatever strength you have.

Can you improve speed and agility without plyometrics? Probably. Will plyometrics enhance your training program? Probably. And since we are not exactly sure what works, we might as well take full advantage of everything out there that is safe and productive. We know that plyos can be safe if done properly; they (like just about anything) can also be dangerous if used incorrectly. We also know they have helped improve performance in many research studies. So, plyos are similar to other training modalities in that they might help an athlete even if used incorrectly, but they elicit the best results when used properly. Our goal, then, is to understand how to most effectively use them to improve speed and agility.

Proper Use of Plyometrics

A lot of people believe that plyometrics will magically enhance straight-ahead speed because track coaches use them with some of the fastest people on earth. Besides all of the scientific literature about plyometrics, there is a great deal of anecdotal evidence that suggests plyos will help straight-ahead speed. Yet, a properly implemented plyometric program has the potential to improve multi-directional agility even more so than straight-ahead speed.

One excellent use for plyos is to teach proper lower body mechanics in sport movements. Many young athletes, especially females, exhibit flawed lower body mechanics in COD movements, and plyos can be used to train body control and alignment. A common issue for many athletes is an unsafe valgus moment created at the knee when the body is lowered into a squat-type position, such as landing from a jump, or decelerating the body during a COD (see Fig. 7.1). There are many possible reasons for this problem, including strength deficiencies and anatomical considerations; but a properly implemented plyometric program has the potential to teach an athlete the body control necessary to improve this condition.

Many programs are now being developed with the goal of improving landing technique. Therapists, doctors, coaches and biomechanists are now trying to teach athletes how to absorb shock and control the body when landing from a jump. Improper landings are responsible for many injuries, and the programs are showing good results. The main points that should be stressed when coaching proper landings are:

Fig. 7.1 Landing from a jump with unsafe valgus moment at knee

- Absorb the shock with the ankles, knees and hips.
- Land toe-to-heel.
- Maintain proper knee alignment.
- Keep feet wide to improve balance and stability.
- Land in an athletic position with the hips, knees and ankles bent, weight distributed on the entire foot, and a slight forward body lean with the chest up. See Fig. 7.2

Certain plyo exercises can also help athletes feel more comfortable in the "low and wide" position used in directional changes. For many athletes, proper body positioning feels awkward, difficult, and even a little scary. Plyo drills like the 4-square sequences and dot drills help athletes get used to bending the knees during different movements. Again, if good coaching is not present, many of the benefits derived from plyometrics may be lost.

Other reasons for utilizing plyometrics include the stimulation of the nervous system and the development of eccentric strength that is so important to optimal agility performance. Since the goal of plyometric training is to improve power, these drills should always be done when the athlete is relatively fresh and motivated to give maximal effort. Doing plyos in a fatigued state, or with sub-maximal effort will severely compromise the potential results of a plyometric training program.

Because many plyometric exercises place a great deal of stress on the body, it is important to keep the workouts relatively short, with long (1-3 minutes) rest periods, and an emphasis on

Fig. 7.2 Safe landing from a jump

intensity. The shock of intense plyometric drills can lead to overuse injuries such as patellar or Achilles tendonitis if the volume of work, or number of foot contacts, is too high. Just like speed and agility work, quality is much more important that quantity. In fact, focusing on quantity can actually have a detrimental effect.

Many Americans like to subscribe to the "more is better" point of view. Unfortunately, when the goal is to improve athletic explosiveness, the human body does not respond well to high volumes of work. The key is to figure out the minimum amount of work necessary to elicit the optimal result. No one knows exactly what this volume is, but overtraining with plyometrics is a common problem for many athletes. When training the nervous system, quality is always much more important than quantity, so be sure to keep the intensity high and the volume relatively low.

There are more complete texts available on the subject of plyometrics, but the purpose of this book is to provide basic scientific information and teach the reader practical uses for different training modalities.

Plyometric Training Guidelines

- Progress from low-intensity to high-intensity drills, but do not progress until the lower level drills are mastered. There is no reason to perform advanced drills if the rudimentary drills cannot be performed with excellent technique. When in doubt, progress very slowly. Even low-intensity drills will elicit results, so slow down, and concentrate on movement quality.
- Allow relatively long rest periods between sets, with longer rest periods required for more intense drills. Low-impact drills will require shorter rest periods, but the recovery must be long enough to allow the athlete to execute the next set with proper technique. Remember, plyos are not meant to be used as a conditioning drill; plyos are meant to enhance nervous-system function. There are more appropriate ways to enhance aerobic or anaerobic fitness.
- There is no specific age or strength level necessary to begin a plyo program, but the athlete must have enough body control and strength to perform the drills with proper technique. If the athlete is unable to demonstrate adequate technique, it is recommended that the drill not be used. Many professionals recommend athletes be able to squat 1½ times their bodyweight before engaging in plyometrics. This is a decent guideline, but it is rather arbitrary. The point is to have sufficient strength to control the forces encountered during landings. This is often very subjective, so when in doubt, slow down. Younger athletes can engage is low-impact plyo drills if they have the strength and body control to perform proper technique. Below age 14 (in most cases) the focus should be on refining motor skills, so there is no real need to use high-impact plyometric drills.
- Large and/or young athletes generally should not engage in high-impact drills. The risk of injury is not worth the potential benefits.
- Choose drills that mimic sport-specific movement patterns whenever possible. Practicing the exact movements used in competition should be a high priority, with plyometric drills utilized to supplement the sport-specific training.
- When introducing a new drill into a program, start slowly. There is no reason to advance too quickly.
- Perform plyometric drills early in the training session when you are relatively fresh and motivated to perform the drills with maximal effort.

- Limit the amount of plyometric training when an athlete is engaged in a high volume of work or practice. Pre-season and in-season training programs should include a reduced volume of plyometric work because the physical demands on the athlete are already very high.
- Allow adequate recovery time between plyometric workouts. This will vary depending on the intensity of the training session, but no more than two workouts per week are necessary in most situations. Because of the demands plyometrics place on the nervous system, a great deal of time is required for full recovery. Plyometrics should not be performed every day.
- Concentrate on proper landings. Jumping in the air is not nearly as demanding as landing, so an emphasis should be placed on using proper landing technique.
- Incorporate aggressive arm swing into jumps with a major vertical component. The arms will begin behind the body, and will be forcefully swung upward to create momentum as the hips, ankles and knees extend. Proper arm swing can greatly enhance jumping ability.

Common Mistakes With Plyometrics

- Inadequate intensity and rest periods. Optimally, the intensity will be as high as possible, and the rest periods will be relatively long. Give 1-3 minutes between the most intense sets to ensure optimal effort. If sub-maximal effort is used as a result of fatigue from improper rest periods, the effectiveness of the training will be compromised. Many athletes will feel uncomfortable with long rest periods because they are not accustomed to this, but adequate rest periods are imperative.
- Performing too many reps per set. Most intense plyometric drills such as squat-jumps, bounds, or long jumps should be performed in sets of 4-10 reps. Lower-impact drills such as 4-square or dot drills can be performed in sets of up to 40 reps. Sets can also be timed for the lower-impact drills. 5-20 seconds per set is appropriate for most exercises. One-legged drills will typically have shorter durations than two-legged drills.
- Poor technique. Proper knee bend and body alignment must be a priority in all plyometric drills. The athlete must be able to land softly and under control from any jumping drill. Watch for an exaggerated valgus moment at the knee, especially in females.
- Rushing progression. Many coaches have unprepared athletes perform high-level plyometrics because they assume the more difficult drills will elicit greater results. This is a mistake because an athlete who is not prepared to perform a drill will simply reinforce faulty mechanics or increase the risk of injury. Take your time, and progress slowly to more intense drills. A more demanding drill will only help an athlete who is ready for it.
- Using plyometrics for fitness conditioning. While there can be an anaerobic training effect from some plyometric drills, the goal is to improve neuromuscular efficiency, not condition an athlete. There are much safer and more efficient drills to accomplish this.
- Using plyos at the wrong time. A fatigued athlete should not perform most plyometric drills, and they should not be utilized when sport practice includes a great deal of jumping or pounding. Include plyometrics near the beginning of a workout, and at a time of the training year that allows for optimal recovery.
- Using plyos with the wrong people. Young athletes or those with inadequate strength should not be rushed into plyometrics. It is unnecessary and can reinforce inefficient movement patterns. Caution should also be used with large athletes whose bodyweight will create a great deal of force on the body during landing or deceleration.

Squat Jumps: Can be performed holding the landings or with repeated jumps. Add a weight vest or dumbbells for added resistance. This is a basic plyo drill that can be used by most athletes. Work on approach jumps by taking one large step forward before the jump.

Long Jumps: Same comments as Squat Jumps (above). Progress to one-leg jumps as the athlete masters the landing technique.

Box Jumps: Begin by only jumping on to the box. Progress to jumping on and off repeatedly. One leg jumps can be done on very low (6") boxes. Increase the height of the box as long as technique is sound.

Lateral Box Hops: Jump repeatedly side to side over an obstacle. Start with a low obstacle and increase the height as needed. Jumps should be performed in multiple directions over the obstacle for overall development.

Skaters: Hop laterally over an obstacle (a ball in the picture). No weight is placed on the obstacle. The emphasis is on the lateral movement, springing off the ground quickly.

Bounding: This a fairly advanced drill that will help increase stride length. Jump off of one foot and land on the other. Begin by holding the landings and progress to multiple bounds as quick and far as possible.

Lateral Bounding: Jump laterally (or diagonally) off of one foot and land on the other. Begin by holding the landings and progress to quick bounds. This is an excellent drill for developing power and quickness in agility movements.

4-Square Pattern

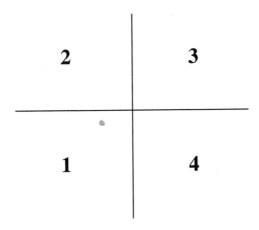

The following drills can be performed with 1 foot or 2 feet:

1-2
1-4
1-3
2-4
1-2-3
1-3-2
1-2-3-4
4-3-2-1
1-3-2-4

Add a 6-12" "channel" between each number to create longer jumps. This will require the feet to travel farther from the center of gravity, which will more closely resemble COD movements.

Add a 6-12" obstacle between each number that the athlete must jump over. This will enhance the vertical component of the exercise.

Attempt to stay low with the knees bent in an effort to simulate COD mechanics. Only add a barrier or space between the numbers when proper mechanics are mastered in the basic drill.

Dot Drills

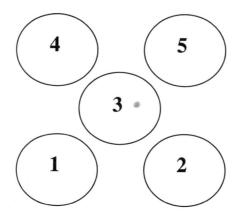

A single number means the jump is performed with both feet on the same dot unless denoted as a single leg drill. Hyphenated numbers mean that one foot is on each number simultaneously. "Turn" means you twist 180° and continue. Like the 4-Square patterns, work on body control and maintaining knee-bend during each change of direction.

1. 1-2, 3, 4-5
2. 4-5, 3, 1-2, 3
3. 5, 3, 2, 3
4. 4, 3, 1, 3
5. 1, 2
6. 1, 3, 4, 3, 5, 3, 2, 3, 1
7. 1-2, 3, Turn, 4-5, 3, Turn, 1-2
8. 1, 2, 5, 4, 1
9. 4, 3, 2, 3
10. 1, 3, 2, 3
11. 4, 3, 5, 3
12. Any variation of these drills can be done one foot at a time.

Chapter 7 Coaching Tip

When implementing your plyometric program, create drills that combine jumping, running and CODs to create the most realistic, or sport-specific, drills possible. This may ultimately be the best use of plyometrics to enhance sport performance. For example, begin an agility drill with a vertical jump or long jump, followed directly by a sprint requiring acceleration. Or, design drills that include starting, stopping, changes of direction and jumping. Creativity is the key to making a training program effective and maintain long-term interest.

An excellent combination drill is called the Jump-Sprint. Begin the drill with a squat jump. Upon landing, sprint 5-10 yards and come to a complete stop as quickly as possible. Hold an athletic position briefly before repeating the jump and sprint. Many variations of this drill can be created by changing the direction in which the athlete runs after landing. Another variation is to rotate 90-360° during each jump. Rotation during the jump will challenge the athlete's proprioception (ability to know where the body is in space) and may enhance an athlete's ability to land safely from a jump.

Notes

Chapter 8

Safe & Efficient Strength Development

The first thing that must be understood about strength training for speed and agility is that there are no magic exercises that absolutely *must* be done to improve performance. Anyone that tells you that a certain exercise is an absolute must is simply propagating myths. There is not one shred of scientific evidence to support this kind of statement. Let me say it again, there are no magical exercises or training modalities that *must* be done to improve speed and agility. If there were, everyone would know about them and the benefits would be unquestioned.

It is important to remember that the goal of traditional strength training (in this discussion, strength training does not include plyometrics) is simply to improve strength. Because it has been shown that improving stride length is so important to speed development, strength training is vital to enhancing the body's ability to apply force into the ground on each step. The tension applied to a muscle during training forces the body to adapt and become stronger. To make significant improvements in strength takes a long time, but once an athlete's strength has improved, it can increase his/her potential to execute sport skills faster or with more force. A reduction in sports-related injuries is also a major benefit of engaging in a well-rounded strength-training program, and should be at the top of anyone's list of training priorities.

Properly training sport skills through practice and movement training is clearly the most effective way to improve speed and agility, but strength training will add a valuable physical trait that can positively impact the performance potential of many athletes. It should be noted, however, that many studies have shown that strength training alone is not a very efficient way to improve speed.

There is some debate as to the effectiveness of strength training on sport performance, but the consensus of research in this area shows that it has a significant positive impact. With this in mind, it should be clear that a strength-training program is important, but spending an inordinate amount of time in the weight room does not seem to be a good choice if the goal is speed and agility enhancement. For example, it has been shown that including plyometrics (see Chapter 7) in the training regime seems to elicit much better speed-related results than strength exercises alone. This suggests that some kind of movement training which emphasizes the stretch-shortening cycle should be incorporated into your program for maximum results. It seems that time invested in sport practice or movement training yields a much bigger payoff than time spent lifting weights. A good strength training program for performance enhancement should be as time efficient as possible to allow an athlete to concentrate on sport skills and not over-tax the recovery abilities of the body.

Many athletes engage in a strength-training program to increase muscle mass or bodyweight. This is particularly important for an undersized athlete. In this case, a stronger emphasis may be put on the strength program. Increased muscle mass and strength is important for some sports, but it should be noted that the amount of strength *relative to the athlete's body weight* seems to be much more important to speed and agility than absolute strength. With this in mind, it is important that an athlete strive to gain lean body mass, as opposed to fat mass, when attempting to gain weight. Gaining fat mass is appropriate for some athletes, but it generally does not improve sport performance. Body weight and composition should be monitored in an effort to gain an appropriate amount of weight so as not to overburden the athlete during sport performance.

The forces encountered by the muscles in many sport movements are many times that of an athlete's bodyweight. In a properly performed COD, it takes a tremendous amount of eccentric strength just to decelerate the body before reacceleration in a different direction. And, if an athlete intends to reaccelerate quickly (which is usually the goal), the musculature must create an incredible amount of force in a very short time. Strengthening the lower body and core musculature will give an athlete the potential to slow down, stop, and reaccelerate the body with greater propulsive force.

Studies have shown that strength plays a much larger role in starting and stopping than at top sprint speed. Therefore, strength is extremely important for starts, agility, and fast CODs. Specifically, the gluteus and quadriceps are most important in these situations. The hamstrings have been shown to be more important during a maximal-speed sprint when the body is already moving rapidly. Ultimately, the nervous system is responsible for properly firing in a way that will create an optimal muscular contraction for any given activity. But, an athlete with a strength deficiency just doesn't have the strength available to do the things a stronger athlete is capable of. This is not to say that a stronger athlete is necessarily a better athlete, but increasing an athlete's strength will generally help performance in some way, especially stopping, starting, and changing directions.

Systematic & Progressive Overload

With all of this in mind, the goal of strength training remains very simple: developing strength in the most efficient manner possible. There are many ways to do this – many exercises, many programs, many philosophies and a whole lot of equipment – but, when you strip away all of the hypothetical discussions and scientific jargon, one basic principle remains as the basis for developing strength: systematic and progressive overload.

All you need to do is overload your body by systematically and progressively increasing the demands placed on the musculature. In doing this, the strength of your muscles will gradually increase, raising your potential to create force in any movement. To make this happen, you must constantly attempt to lift more than you are capable of. If you are capable of performing 8 repetitions with 100 pounds today, you must attempt to perform at least 9 repetitions during the next training session. If you never attempt this (or at least perform multiple sets of the exercise to create fatigue), the body has no reason to get stronger.

Your muscles do not get stronger during the workout. On the contrary, the musculature fatigues during training, and at the end of a session you are temporarily weakened. Then, you eat and sleep, and allow the body to recover from the session. If you have adequately stimulated the musculature, your body basically says, "This guy is crazy. What he tried to do was really hard, and I'm tired. I'm going to rebuild these muscles a little stronger than before, so when he tries to lift that weight again, it will be easier for me." That's not the scientific version of strength development, but you get the point.

The goal of each repetition is to recruit and stimulate as many muscle fibers as possible. The goal of a set is to fatigue as many fibers as possible, which will ultimately force them to adapt to the stimulus. If the musculature is not required to do something more difficult than ever before during each training session, it has no reason to change. So, you must systematically and progressively increase the demands placed on the body if progress is to be made.

The most basic way to accomplish this is to attempt at least one more repetition on each set during every training session. Your body will not allow you to improve on every set, every session, but that can be the goal. When you are able to perform a pre-determined number of repetitions on a set (typically 6-12 reps for upper body and 8-15 reps for lower body), you will increase the weight used during the next training session. That is your *system of progression.* Very simple. Very straightforward. And it works. Increasing both the number of repetitions and the weight you use is typically called double progression. Double progression is a version of linear progression, but there is another system of progression called periodization.

Periodization is a much more complicated training system that varies the training intensity in an effort to more effectively stimulate strength adaptations. The research on periodization is not conclusive, but there seems to be some evidence that it may be able to improve strength slightly better than linear progression in some situations. However, for simplicity, using linear progression to help improve your strength for optimal speed and agility is a very straightforward and efficient way to train. There are several books dedicated to periodization that can be referred to if you have a desire to learn more about this training philosophy.

Repetitions

No matter how you plan to overload your musculature, the foundation of strength training is the proper performance of a single repetition. Performing perfect reps increases the effectiveness of every workout. The purpose of a properly performed repetition is to produce tension in the muscle which, when performed repeatedly, will cause **muscular fatigue**. In order to achieve the proper tension and resulting fatigue, one must consider three factors: speed of movement, body position and leverage, and constant tension. There are some cases when these principles do not apply, such as using lighter weights at faster speeds in an effort to maximize power output. This will be discussed separately.

Speed of Movement

The speed at which a movement is performed should minimize momentum. The weight should be lifted slowly and under control, and it should take 1-2 seconds to lift the weight. At the mid-range of the exercise (when the muscles are fully contracted), the lifter should briefly pause (weight stack, dumbbell, barbell, body, etc. should remain stationary). After the brief pause, the lowering phase occurs, lasting 3-5 seconds. As with the lifting phase, the lowering phase should be performed deliberately and in a controlled manner. If using a weight-stack device, the weights should not bang together at the end of the repetition.

Body Position and Leverage

Using leverage decreases the difficulty of an exercise. For example, arching the back when performing the bench press or bicep curl improves leverage, allowing more weight to be lifted. Similarly, moving the seat further back when performing the leg press also improves leverage. Although more weight is being lifted, this does not necessarily mean that the muscles are getting stronger. The mechanical advantage gained by the increased leverage allows the individual to lift more weight. Because the immediate goal of strength training is to achieve muscular fatigue, an exercise should be difficult to perform, yet safe and comfortable on the joints.

Constant Tension

All repetitions should be performed using a safe, full range of motion, with the muscle constantly loaded. The muscle can be unloaded by resting partway through the repetition, or allowing the weight to accelerate during the lowering phase of the repetition. Allowing the plates to bounce off of the weight stack increases momentum, making it easier to start the next repetition. To maintain constant muscular tension, the weight should be lifted and lowered in a smooth and controlled manner.

Strength-Program Design

Designing strength-training programs may seem very complicated, but it doesn't have to be. Don't turn this into rocket science – it's not. The basic idea is to choose exercises that train all of the major muscles in the body, taking care to balance the strength on all sides of a joint. A good program will have the athlete train as efficiently as possible in an effort to save time and energy for everything else that needs attention (speed, agility, sport skills, conditioning, tactical awareness, etc.). An improperly designed program will require too much time and effort, overtrain the athlete, and can cause muscular imbalances around a joint, eventually leading to injuries or compromised performance. Wasting time or creating unnecessary fatigue will impair an athlete's ability to work on other skills, and will often lead to a decrease in motivation to train. Overtraining is as common as undertraining. Keep the workouts brief (less than one hour), and focus on intensity. For stimulating athletic strength gains, quality is much more important than quantity.

The equipment you have available is relatively inconsequential to increasing your strength. Most strength training equipment allows you to gradually increase the load in a safe manner. This does not mean that all strength equipment is safe or manufactured with perfect ergonomics, but there are so many safe and efficient alternatives that this should not impede your progress. In fact, a basic set of free weights will allow you to build as much strength as you'll ever need. If you are fortunate enough to have access to specialized equipment, consider yourself lucky and take advantage of it whenever possible.

Exercise Selection: Choose 1-3 exercises for each body part, keeping in mind that many exercises involve multiple muscles. It is a good idea to choose exercises that train the same muscle in a slightly different way. For example, the bench press and incline press both work the chest, shoulders and triceps, but the tension is placed on the musculature at a slightly different angle. To optimize the function and safety of each joint, attack each muscle group from different angles. It is not necessary to use multiple angles during each workout; you can vary the angles from workout to workout.

Choose at least one exercise for every major body part to ensure overall development. Also, be sure to balance the amount of work done on each side of a joint. For every set that strengthens one side of a joint, another should be performed on the opposite side of the joint. For example, each set of quadriceps work (knee extension) should be countered with a set of hamstring work (knee flexion). This is a simple example, but the idea is to develop balanced strength throughout the body to ensure optimal function.

While there is limited scientific evidence to support the transfer of weight-room power to sport movement, it may be beneficial to include a safe lower-body "power" exercise 1-2 times per week. Examples of these exercises are: weighted squat-jumps, high pulls, power shrugs, plyometric exercises, and resisted speed and agility drills. These exercises will use a weight between 10-30% of maximum strength and should always be light enough to allow for maximum velocity. Including one or more of these exercises in your program may help develop power, and it is *possible* that this could be useful in sport movements. Although there is no direct scientific evidence suggesting these exercises transfer to on-field skills, it should be noted that many experts utilize similar methods as part of an overall speed-development program.

Sets: Perform 1-3 sets of each exercise. Limit the number of sets so that the intensity can stay high. This will keep the workouts brief and efficient. There are numerous studies that provide evidence that a limited number of sets produces the same results as performing multiple sets of each exercise. Many people are not capable of performing maximal intensity on every set, however, so performing multiple sets of some exercises is a common way to more completely fatigue the muscles involved in each exercise. There is also some evidence that suggests a higher training volume at certain times of the year may be very beneficial to strength gains. Strategically increasing training volume at certain times may be beneficial. Consistently performing more than 20 total sets per workout is not recommended for most athletes as it appears to lower the intensity of each training session and can lead to over training complications.

Reps: As long as you are systematically and progressively overloading the musculature, the number of repetitions is not incredibly important. However, there is some evidence suggesting that heavier weight with lower reps (1-6) is optimal for maximal strength gains, while a slightly higher number of reps (8-15) is optimal for hypertrophy, or muscular growth. Both of these ranges will elicit both strength and size gains, and both are effective for sport performance. Because heavy weight takes a heavier toll on the body, and can potentially be more dangerous for some exercises, a more moderate weight is often recommended. There is no need to work with maximal weights, unless the athlete is preparing for a powerlifting competition. And, even in this case, maximal weights do not need to be used with great frequency. Most sets should end in momentary muscular fatigue somewhere between 6-15 reps, but it is OK to include some heavier and lighter work.

Younger athletes who have not yet reached puberty typically have no reason to use heavy weights. Most recommendations suggest ranges of 10-20 reps for pre-pubescent athletes. If the weight is too heavy to perform ten good repetitions, a lighter weight should be used. Strength training does not appear to be dangerous for young athletes. On the contrary, many experts agree that a good training program can help young athletes lower the potential for injury. The lighter weight is used to help the athletes concentrate on proper technique and execution of each repetition.

Rest Between Sets: It appears that 1-3 minutes rest between sets allows for sufficient recovery during a workout. Research suggests that a longer rest period is optimal for building maximal strength, while short rest periods are optimal for hypertrophy. In an effort to maintain efficiency, it is generally recommended that no more than two minutes be taken between most sets.

Training Frequency: Most athletes should perform intense strength training 2-4 days per week, working each muscle group on non-consecutive days. While there is a great deal of interest in finding the optimal training schedule, most training schedules are more influenced by time availability and logistics than physiology. The key here is to leave approximately 48-72 hours between training the same body parts.

For convenience, many athletes utilize one of the following training programs:
- Total body workouts: M-W-F, T-Th-Sat, or only twice per week.
- Upper Body on Mon & Thurs, Lower Body on Tues & Fri.
- Alternating Upper & Lower Body workouts on M-W-F. This program trains each body part three times every two weeks.

All of these options have proven to be effective routines for many athletes. Training only once per week (on a consistent basis) does not seem to provide enough stimulation for most people. Training more than four days per week seems to over-stress the recovery abilities of most people, especially when additional training (speed & agility, sport practice, conditioning, etc.) is performed.

Sample Strength-Training Routines

Here are some examples of well-rounded routines for upper body, lower body, core, and total body using basic exercises. Multiple exercises on one line means that one of the exercises should be chosen during each workout. The exercises are relatively interchangeable, and work the muscles from slightly different angles.

Lower Body

Exercise	Reps
Squat/Deadlift/Leg Press	15
Squat/Deadlift/Leg Press	10
Squat/Deadlift/Leg Press	6-10
RDL	10-15
RDL	8-12
Hip Flexion/Extension	8-12
Hip Abduction/Adduction	8-12
Leg Curl	8-12
Calf Raise	15-20
Calf Raise	10-15
Lunges/1-Leg Leg Press	10-15

Upper Body

Exercise	Reps
Bench Press/Incline Press	10
Bench Press/Incline Press	8
Bench Press/Incline Press	4-6
Chins	Max
Incline Press/DB Press/Dips	8-12
Row/Pulldown	8-12
Row/Pulldown	6-10
Standing Military Press	8-12
Lateral Raise	8-12
Bent Over Raise/Tube Pull	10-15
Shrugs	10-15

Total Body

Exercise	Reps
Squat/Deadlift/Leg Press	15
Squat/Deadlift/Leg Press	10
Squat/Deadlift/Leg Press	6-8
RDL/Leg Curl	10-15
RDL/Leg Curl	6-10
Calf Raise	10-15
Bench Press/Incline Press	8-12
Chin-Up/Pull-Up/Pulldown	8-12
Bench Press/Incline Press	6-10
Row	8-12
Lateral Raise	8-12
Sit Ups	10-20
Twists	20-40
Back Extension	10-15

Core

Exercise	Reps
Hanging Leg Raise	15
Incline Sit-Ups	15
Back Extension	15
Side Core Hold	30 sec. each side
Prone Marches	40

Obviously, there are dozens of additional exercises and routines to choose from that are all effective ways to stimulate strength gains. Discussing the intricacies of all of these modalities and routines is well beyond the scope of this book, but there are many books dedicated specifically to strength training. As stated earlier, strength is being discussed here because of its importance to improving speed and agility performance. If the principles covered here are applied on a consistent basis, massive amounts of strength can be developed. It does not need to be confusing.

Ankle Conditioning

Because such extreme demands are placed on the ankle during agility work, special care should be taken to enhance the function of this area. This does not take a tremendous amount of time, but the effort may help reduce the risk of injury as well as improve sport performance.

The first consideration is properly warming up the ankle. A complete warm up routine should include some kind of ankle rolls/circles to dynamically activate the musculature in the lower leg. If there is a history of ankle injuries or shin splints, toe taps and bodyweight toe raises can be added to the routine. The rest of the warm up routine should prepare the ankle for training, but you may even want to add a few quick response jumps like the 4-square plyometric drill to focus on ankle preparation.

If there is no acute injury, and ankle conditioning is a concern, the 4-square drill is an excellent way to train the lower leg and ankle. Working through different patterns allows the ankle and foot to learn sound mechanics and may improve proprioception, or body control.

Another ankle strengthening exercise that can even be used to rehabilitate an injury is the Stork Drill (see page 141). This drill begins by simply standing on one foot. For some athletes, this will be demanding. Once this can easily be done for at least 30 seconds, the athlete's balance can be challenged, which will more fully engage the lower leg and foot musculature to maintain balance. This can be done in a number of ways including having a partner throw a ball or medicine ball to the athlete. The ball should be thrown so the athlete's balance is tested. Throw high, low, and to the sides so the center of gravity is displaced often. This can also be done alone by simple knocking yourself off balance through twisting and reaching. A bit of imagination can really enhance the effectiveness of this drill. Perform these drills once or twice a week for 2-4 minutes to keep the ankles functioning optimally.

To increase the difficulty, the Stork Drill can be performed on foam mats, rollers, or a mini-trampoline. This will simply increase the demands placed on the ankle to maintain balance. While this seems like a very simple drill, most athletes will feel the lower leg musculature working extremely hard to maintain balance. It is important to remember that the balance gained from performing these exercises will not necessarily improve agility or sport performance. These drills are simply intended to strengthen the musculature. Agility work must always be included at some point to stimulate the specific neural pathways used in sport movement.

Olympic Weightlifting

There are coaches who have suggested that the Olympic lifts (clean, jerk, and snatch) must be used to develop explosive athletic power. Because the execution of these lifts requires a great deal of strength in a short period of time, some coaches have decided that they must create powerful athletes. Taking this one step further, some coaches have claimed that these lifts are absolutely essential to creating explosive athletes.

While there is scientific literature that supports the inclusion of lighter weight (typically 30% of maximum strength) exercises performed at fast speeds to improve power, there are safer and more time-efficient ways to accomplish this besides the Olympic lifts. These lifts (or any exercise for that matter) can certainly develop strength and power, but there are several practical reasons not to use them with most athletes. This section is not meant to bash the Olympic lifts or anyone who uses them. The lifts have merit and, if taught properly, can be an excellent addition to some programs. The goal here is to explain that they are not absolutely necessary or as superior as many coaches claim. There are many other ways to elicit the same, or better, results that are safer and easier for athletes to perform. The following is a brief overview. For more detailed information, please refer to Chapters 19 & 20 (Kielbaso and Wakeham) in *Maximize Your Training*.

- The Olympic lifts are extremely technical. Competitive weightlifters dedicate their lives to the proper execution of these lifts. Olympic lifting is a sport, and the proper execution of the lifts takes a tremendous amount of time and effort. The time and effort spent learning these lifts is not proportional to the possible benefits they may elicit. This time and effort could be used in much more productive ways.
- Flawed technique in any of the lifts can lead to injuries. Technical mistakes even have the potential to acutely (and sometimes severely) injure an athlete. Injuries are commonly seen in the wrist, elbow, shoulder, and lower back. Even the proper execution of the lifts has been shown to be potentially dangerous. Several studies have shown that the use of these lifts leads to lower-back pathologies. Even among experienced lifters, the incidence of low back pathology is greatly increased when these lifts are consistently performed.
- Most coaches simply do not have the expertise to properly teach these lifts. Of course, there are fully qualified coaches out there, but are you one of them? If not, you should not be teaching the lifts to your athletes. If a certified and experienced instructor is present, the effectiveness and safety of these lifts improves dramatically. If you feel that these lifts must be included in your program, excellent coaching is mandatory. Sub-par coaching and instruction can lead to injuries and law suits. If you're not qualified, it's just not worth it. It takes a tremendous amount of talent and coaching skill to adequately coach these lifts. If you have a qualified coach available to you, consider yourself very lucky.
- Even if there is a qualified coach teaching the lifts, is there adequate supervision to ensure that all athletes will receive proper instruction? In most situations, there are simply not enough qualified coaches for all the athletes involved. As stated above, the lifts are so technical that a qualified instructor should be supervising every rep of every athlete performing an Olympic lift. There are many qualified instructors who have recognized that it is impossible to properly supervise every athlete. Unless qualified instructors are available for all athletes, a safer alternative may be a good decision.
- There is absolutely no scientific evidence that suggests Olympic weightlifting movements improve speed or agility better than any other training method suggested in this book. The science is simply not there. Hypothetically, the high velocities used in the lifts may help improve power production, but without sound scientific evidence that these complicated lifts will work better than anything else, why spend the time and energy trying to include them in your program?
- While these exercises include the triple extension of the ankle, knee and hip, they do not provide specific movement practice for any sport movement other than Olympic weightlifting. As stated

above, these movements are extremely complex and require a great deal of practice to perfect. An analysis of the movement shows that these lifts do not mimic any other sport movement, so they are not "specific" training for any athlete other than a weightlifter. Sport-specific movement patterns need to be practiced through movement training, while strength training is intended to develop strength. Strength-training movements utilize different movement speeds, joint angles, neural pathways, joint velocities, and muscular recruitment patterns than movements utilized on the field or court. When any of these differences are present, the skill transfer is severely limited.

- The methods suggested in this book are generally safer and more efficient than trying to include Olympic lifts in your program.

These lifts may have a place in performance training, but their applicability to sport performance is not nearly as great as purported by some coaches. If the claims of their superiority were absolutely true, there would be a clear and noticeable trend of superior athletic ability in athletes who consistently utilize them versus those who do not. However, professional football scouts still describe certain athletes as slow-footed, non-explosive, or lacking speed even after consistent use of these lifts for 4-8 years. The same scouts sometimes describe athletes who have never used the Olympic lifts as fast, explosive, quick or powerful.

If Olympic lifts were absolutely necessary for the development of speed and power, and they worked better than anything else (as many coaches have claimed), we would never hear scouts make statements like these. It would not be possible. The truth is, many training methods work as long as a system of progressive overload is applied and a solid movement training program is utilized. There is nothing magical about the Olympic lifts or any other training modality, so don't waste your time searching for the Holy Grail of strength and power development; it does not exist.

If you love the Olympic lifts, are qualified to teach them, and can provide adequate supervision for all athletes, including them in your program may be appropriate. If not, there are safe and effective alternatives to accomplish the same results. The following is a list of safer and less complicated alternatives that are all designed to improve power, thus replacing the Olympic lifts:

- Plyometrics
- Weighted Plyometrics – using weight vests, dumbbells or specialized equipment
- Squat-Jumps - using dumbbells or weight vests
- Medicine Balls
- Agility Drills with weighted vests or resistive tubing
- Weighted Sleds
- Power Shrugs
- Speed Squats
- High Pulls

Each one of these exercises accomplishes the same goal of an Olympic Lift without the complexity, safety concerns, or need for extraordinary coaching skills. Including one or more of these exercises in your training program may help you develop lower-body power in a sensible way.

Strength Training Exercises

The following section is not intended to give in-depth information on the intricacies of every strength-training exercise. The pictures illustrate proper technique, but it is assumed that the reader has a basic understanding of strength training and his/her limitations. All of the exercises shown are safe and effective choices, but they may not be appropriate for everyone in every situation. Be sure to consult with a professional before engaging in these, or any other, exercises.

This section is not intended to be a complete text, so it is highly recommended to consult other sources for more information on this important aspect of training if a deeper understanding is desired. There are many other exercises and modalities that are safe and effective, but this section will certainly give the reader the necessary information to develop an excellent program.

Chapter 8 Coaching Tip

One of the more difficult aspects of developing strength is the fact that it takes a great deal of time, dedication, and patience. Progress is made very slowly, and because of this, it is easy to lose focus. To help fight boredom and burnout, try the following:

1. Vary the workouts. This doesn't mean that the routine needs to change every day or even every week. You can insert a totally different workout every couple of weeks just to mix things up and keep the athlete's interest. That workout needs to be very different than the normal routine so it is a clear break from the monotony. This workout does not need to be scientific or "perfect;" it just needs to be interesting enough to make the athletes enjoy themselves and possibly even talk about it afterward. It may include some silly workouts such as carrying each other around the track, pushing cars around the parking lot, or doing hundreds of reps in a competition to see who can do the most. Holidays (even the little ones like Veteran's Day) are a great excuse to throw in a crazy workout.

2. Keep the atmosphere exciting. Creating this environment requires you to understand what the athlete's like, not necessarily what you like. You might love to listen to heavy metal while you lift, but the athletes might hate it. Don't force your preferences on them. It's hard enough for an athlete to push himself to the limit every day. There is no reason not to make it enjoyable whenever possible.

3. Use surprise days off. Every once in a while, a strategically planned surprise day off can really boost morale and inject enthusiasm in the following workouts. Keep in mind that a consistent schedule will elicit the best long-term results, but there are times when taking a day off makes a much bigger difference than any workout would. Especially during the pre-season, or time of year when the workouts have been extremely intense, always be aware of giving the athletes enough time to fully recover. Nothing will sabotage a season like overtraining or burn out. And, the only way to fight that is to be keenly aware of attitudes, morale, and recovery. Finally, if you're going to give the athletes a day off, tell them a day in advance. This gives them time to enjoy it and even plan on doing something enjoyable. The point of the day off is to let the athlete recover, have a little fun, and rejuvenate – so give them time to make plans and fully enjoy the down time.

Deadlift (Quads & Glutes) - Excellent overall lower-body exercise. Traditionally performed with a barbell, but can be done with dumbbells as shown on the right. The most common error is poor posture (not maintaining a slight arch in the lower back), which can lead to serious back problems. Never allow the lower back to "round over."

Squats (Quads & Glutes) - Similar to the deadlift, but the weight is placed on the shoulders. Always maintain a slight arch in the lower back. Descend as low as possible, but stop when the pelvis begins to rotate. Getting the thighs parallel to the ground is a good goal, but this is not appropriate for many athletes. A long femur and poor flexibility will make it very difficult to get this low.

Romanian Deadlift - RDL (Glutes & Hamstrings) - Also known as straight (or stiff) leg deadlifts. This exercise typically requires a great deal of practice to perform correctly, but it is a great selection for glute/ham development. Be sure to maintain a slight arch in the lower back and keep all of the movement at the hips (a rounded back can lead to injury). Only lower the bar to a position that allows you to maintain proper posture with a slight stretch in the hamstrings. You may be able to descend deeper than in the picture, but lowering too deep can lead to problems if posture is not maintained.

Leg Press (Quads & Glutes) - Excellent alternative to the squat or deadlift, and requires much less skill to perform. Depending on the equipment design, the leg press will also take the pressure (compressive force and stability requirements) off the lower back. The seat position should always be properly adjusted. Seek assistance if unsure of proper positioning because this will vary greatly depending on the brand of equipment. The leg press can also be performed one leg at a time for unilateral development.

Lunges (Quads & Glutes) - Great alternative to the squat, and trains each leg independently. This is very "specific" to speed and agility training. Keep the front heel on the ground and the knee over the foot during the descent.

Leg Curl (Hamstrings) - Requires very little coordination, which means most athletes can execute this movement. Be sure to hold the weight at the top of the movement. Align the center of the knee joint with the machine's axis of rotation.

Hip Flexion (Hip Flexors) - The hip flexors help create knee drive, so this is an excellent exercise to assist this motion. Keep the entire body still; only the hip should move. The hip will line up with the machine's axis of rotation, but consult with a professional for proper positioning, depending on the machine.

Hip Extension (Glutes & Hamstrings) - Strengthens the glutes and hamstrings in a motion very similar to sprinting.

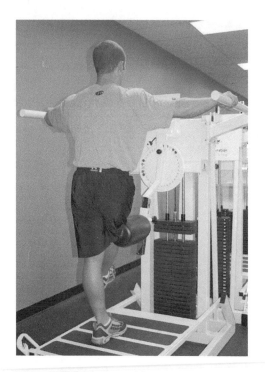 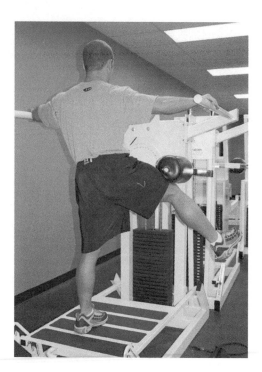

Hip Abduction (Outer Thigh) - Keep the hips parallel to the ground as the thigh is raised.

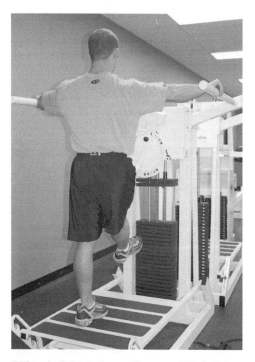 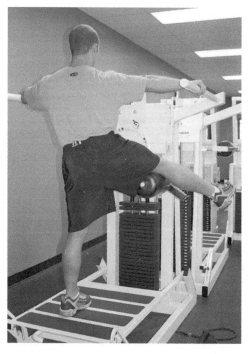

Hip Adduction (Inner Thigh) - Keep the hips parallel to the ground, and only cross the body slightly with the working leg. Inner thigh work is extremely important for many athletes who have strong abductors, but limited adductor work.

Abduction with tubing (Outer Thigh) - Excellent alternative to Hip Abduction when a machine is not available.

Toe Raise (Calves) - Raise as high as possible onto the 1st and 2nd toes. Hold at the top. Do not rest the heel on the ground at the bottom.

Adduction on Slide Board (Inner Thigh) - Excellent groin exercise. May need to pull up with the hands when beginning this exercise. Add internal rotation of the hips (toes rotate from pointed out to pointed in as the legs pull together) for a variation.

Incline Dumbbell Press (Chest, Anterior Deltoid, Triceps) - Presses can be performed on a flat, incline or decline bench with either dumbbells or a barbell (i.e. bench press). There are also many machines that mimic this movement. Each angle will train the musculature in a slightly different way. Lower the weight until the upper arms are slightly past parallel to the ground.

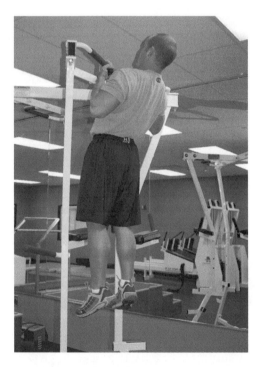

Chin-Up (Lats & Biceps) - If this is too difficult, simply work on the negative portion of the exercise. Step up to the top position, remove the feet, hold at the top, and lower as slowly as possible. Turn the hands around for a pull-up to work the musculature in a slightly different way.

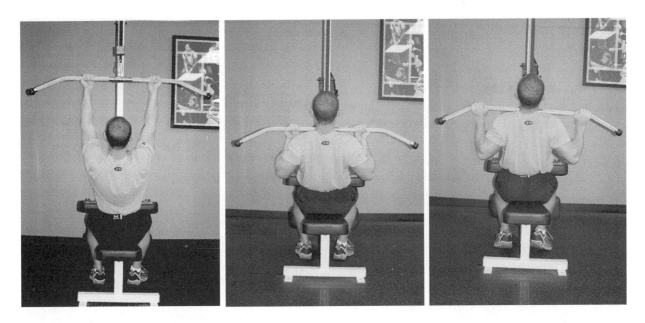

Pull-down (Lats & Biceps) - Excellent alternative to the chin-up or pull-up. Use an underhand grip to involve the biceps more. If using a pronated grip (palms facing away), place the hands where the elbows would meet the bar if the arms were extended to the sides. In both varitions, attempt to pull the shoulder blades back and down as the bar travels toward the chest. Pulling behind the neck is not typically recommended as it offers no advantage and can be potentially dangerous for the shoulder.

Row (Lats) - As the weight is pulled toward the body, pull the shoulder blades back and down. Pause at the top of the movement before lowering under control.

Military Press (Anterior Delts, Triceps) - Lower the weight just below the chin. Maintain good posture throughout the movement or support the back by sitting down with a back rest.

Lateral Raise (Medial Delts) - Raise the weight to slightly past parallel to the ground. Hold at the top and lower slowly. Stop lowering just before the weights touch the body to maintain tension. Keep the shoulder blades pinched back and down, and lean slightly forward at the waist.

Bent-Over Raise (Posterior Delts) - Use light weight, and keep the elbows away from the body.

Shrugs (Traps) - Pull shoulders straight upward. Rotating the shoulders does nothing additional for the traps.

Stork Drill (Ankle) - Excellent drill to activate the lower-leg musculature. Challenge your balance by twisting and changing your COG level. Have a partner throw a ball to you or simply move around on your own.

Sit-Ups (Abdominals) - Attempt to tilt the pelvis so the low back is flat before curling the body upward. "Unroll" the back on the descent so the low back hits the pad first. Leading with the stomach can be hard on the low back.

Hanging Leg Raise (Abdominals) - Begin by bending the knees and pull them to the chest. Tilt the pelvis as the knees raise to fully engage the abdominals. When it is easy to pull the knees to the chest, attempt to pull the feet all the way up to the hands.

Prone Marches (Abs) - Maintain good posture (no sagging at the midsection), and slowly march your feet, one at a time. Move slowly to maintain control. Begin by simply holding the prone position, without marching the feet, until this can be controlled.

Hyperextension (Low Back, Glutes & Hamstrings) - Start with the hips bent and the head near the ground. Raise the body from the hips until the upper body is slightly past parallel to the ground. Hold briefly at the top before lowering. Add a small twist of the upper body as shown below for a variation. Be sure to return to the center before lowering. Athletes will feel this mainly in the lower back, but the glutes and hamstrings are doing a great deal of work.

Chapter 9

Program Design

When designing a complete training program several factors must be taken into consideration. Some experts will try to simplify program design into three or four factors. Others will fail to take all factors into consideration, rendering the program useless in certain situations. Still others will try to apply a cookie-cutter approach to every situation. Unfortunately, creating the right program for every situation is much more complicated than that.

While this is certainly not rocket science, there are a lot of factors to consider when creating the optimal program for each situation. Some of these factors will carry a lot of weight, while others will be relatively meaningless, but they all need to be examined. The following is a list of factors to consider as you create each program:

1. **Goals/Expectations:** What is the purpose of the training program or session? What are the expectations of the coach? Typically there are multiple goals. During an off-season training program, many athletes want to increase speed at the same time they want to improve strength, body composition and sport-specific skills. It is rare to have an athlete who can concentrate 100% of his/her time and effort on one goal, such as speed, so the goals must be prioritized.

2. **Biomechanics of the Sport:** What movements will be performed in competition? Does the sport emphasize straight-ahead running, agility, shuffling, jumping, physical contact, etc.?

3. **Metabolic Requirements of the Sport:** The energy systems used in the sport must be challenged so that biochemical adaptation can occur, and improved conditioning can be enjoyed. The energy systems involved in sports are: ATP-PC, Anaerobic, and Aerobic. A coach or athlete must understand the requirements of the sport so a program can be designed to enhance sport-specific fitness.

4. **Movement-Skill Status:** How well does the athlete currently move? Is the technique good, average, or poor? This will help you determine how much time will be necessary and what kinds of drills will be used.

5. **Training Status:** What has the athlete been doing? Is he/she in shape? Has he/she been participating in a strength program? How does this athlete compare to the competition?

6. **Injuries:** Are there any injuries or health concerns to consider? This will include both past and present injuries. The potential for common injuries to occur in a particular sport or position should also be considered.

7. **Time:** How much time is available for the session? How much time is available each week? How much time is being spent on other activities such as sport practice? How much time is available to recover from each workout? And how much time is available before competition (days, weeks, months, etc)?

8. **Emotional/Psychological Factors:** How motivated is an athlete to do the necessary work? How dedicated will he/she be to follow through with the program? Will the athlete be able to maintain intensity and focus during every workout, or does he/she typically lose interest rather quickly? Will the athlete be training with teammates or alone? How much work can the athlete take psychologically/emotionally? How might the workouts impact team unity? Are off-field factors influencing on-field focus? All stressors should be taken into consideration such as time spent on homework, practice, social life, family obligations, work, etc.

9. **Training Environment:** What kind of space or equipment is available? Will the workouts be done individually or in a group? How many coaches/trainers will be available for each workout?

All of these factors combine to help the coach design an appropriate program or workout. Without taking all of this information into consideration, the optimal program will not be created for an individual or team. The more information the coach has, the more he/she can tailor the workout to the individual or group. Of course, not all of these factors will matter for every situation, but a good coach will be able to distinguish between what matters and what does not, or what can actually change versus what cannot.

It should be noted that *optimal* does not always mean *perfect*. It may be optimal to spend two hours every day, one-on-one, with a completely motivated athlete. Unfortunately, this probably isn't going to happen very often. Creating the optimal program must begin in reality. Perhaps we should rephrase our goal of creating the optimal program to creating a *realistically optimal* program. The perfect program is the one that takes all factors into consideration *and* is right for the situation.

It is very common to design each workout without regard to the other activities the athlete engages in. Many coaches will disregard the need for recovery and will overtrain athletes just to "kick their butts" every workout. It is easy to break an athlete down, but this is not the optimal way to enhance performance. Creating a situation in which the athlete will thrive and maximally improve performance is a far more important, and difficult, task for a coach.

It is impossible to describe the optimal training routine for every unique situation; a cookie-cutter approach is simply an inappropriate way to design a program. The workouts used for a youth athlete who has several years before any important competition will be extremely different than those used for a football player who has four weeks to prepare for a combine test. A coach must be able to consider all of the factors involved and come up with a training regime that will produce optimal results.

That being said, many programs are still going to look fairly similar. Some people think that every athlete should always have an individualized program, but it is perfectly acceptable to have a standard workout for an entire team, as long as you're flexible enough to make modifications for individual needs. Is it really important to have every player on a soccer team doing a different strength or agility program, or can consistency sometimes enhance the team atmosphere? There are situations when creating individualized programs can lead to jealousy and inconsistency which can have a very negative effect on team unity.

Program Design Tips
The following tips will help you design a program appropriate for your situation:
- Focus on mechanics when there is a great deal of time before it is important to demonstrate the skills. For example, developing sound mechanics should be a high priority for most youth athletes.
- For a combine-type situation, concentrate most of your time and effort practicing the specific skills that will be tested.
- When an athlete is unable to dedicate much time to training, focus on mechanics, and instruct the athlete to spend time on conditioning outside of his/her training sessions.
- Work on speed or practice mechanics when an athlete is fresh. Fatigue will negatively affect technique, which can lead to bad habits.
- When an athlete is fatigued from practices and competitions, it is best to allow time for recovery before intense training is resumed. Shortened training sessions are also an option in this situation.

- Once technique has been taught and practiced, give athletes as many opportunities as possible to practice these skills. If sprint mechanics are being trained, multiple sprints should be completed. If improved agility is the goal, give the athlete as many different drills as possible to work on proper footwork.

- When technique work is being done, rest periods need to be longer; focus on mechanics and intensity. When conditioning is the goal, shorten the rest periods.

- If the season or event is far away, conditioning does not need to be a high priority. Time and energy should be spent on mechanics, strength, and sport skills.

- When the season or event is close (2-6 weeks), technique can still be developed, but there needs to be a much greater emphasis on conditioning. In this case, practice skills early in the training session, and end with conditioning work. Keep in mind that it takes incredible effort and intensity to physically prepare for many sports. It is important to push yourself to the limit if you plan to compete at a high level.

- As much as possible, a coach should try to individualize training sessions and corrective feedback. This is very difficult in team situations, but a little individualized coaching can make a tremendous impact on an athlete.

- During early-stage technique work, keep the drills simple so the athletes can concentrate on proper mechanics and body control. Complex drills change an athlete's focus to the drill rather than the technique.

- As the season or event approaches, select drills and create workouts that allow the athletes to feel success. It is not recommended to introduce new techniques close to an event as this often leads to an initial period of frustration as an athlete develops the new skill. This feeling of frustration is often accompanied by a decrease in self-efficacy which can have a negative impact on performance.

- If training is going to take place on several consecutive days, do not crush the athletes on the first day. While this may be tempting, unless the athletes are in great shape, it will do nothing but create problems in subsequent training sessions. Severely sore and fatigued athletes will train with decreased intensity and technique may be compromised. You will spend the next two days frustrated because you can't get everything accomplished. The only times that crushing athletes on the first day of practice should be considered are when you are trying to make a statement to a team or you are confident they are already in good shape. Just be aware of how this will affect the next few days.

Metabolic Conditioning

Metabolic conditioning can be somewhat confusing to coaches and athletes because there is no easy way to accurately measure game fitness. There are certainly ways to test an athlete's oxygen consumption or aerobic capacity, but actually competing in a sport is quite different than any test.

Far too many coaches still test their athletes on the 2-mile run as the primary test of physical preparation. This is so backwards that it can't even be labeled as "old school" thinking. Besides endurance events such as cross-country running, marathons, or triathlons, there is no sport in which the 2-mile run (or any distance running test) accurately assesses a player's level of physical preparation for competition. Sure, games like soccer and rugby require a great deal of running, but none of it occurs in a straight line at the pace in which a distance run is performed. Running at this pace during a game will result in the athlete getting beat to the ball every time.

Without getting into too many details, the metabolic requirements, biochemical processes and biomechanics are so different during sprinting activities that practicing distance running may actually have a negative impact on performance. This is not to say that athletes should never run distances. The aerobic conditioning gained from paced running can be very beneficial in many sports, but this is grossly overemphasized by many coaches.

A much more appropriate approach to sport conditioning would be to analyze the metabolic requirements of the sport and design conditioning routines that train the proper energy systems, movement patterns, and "rhythm" of the game. It is also a good idea to make conditioning workouts much more demanding than the actual game, so that physically, a competition does not seem as difficult.

Energy Systems
The three main ways the body produces energy for physical activity are:

- ATP-PC System – ATP is basically energy. It is what we use to make us move. And, phosphocreatine (PC) helps makes ATP. This is obviously an abridged version of a complex biochemical issue, but it's really about all we need to understand for our purposes. There is a small amount of ATP stored in our muscles that allows us to make sudden, explosive movements without having to wait for the necessary ATP to be made. Intense activities under about 10 seconds utilize the ATP-PC system to satisfy the energy demands.

  A short sprint like a 40-yard dash would utilize the ATP-PC system to supply the energy to run the race. You can only run at that intense pace for a short distance before you are forced to slow down. You have to slow down because your body cannot produce energy fast enough to keep up with the demands being placed upon it. There is only a small amount of ATP stored in the body at any given time, so when it has been used up, your body has to manufacture more. We cannot manufacture ATP fast enough to supply the muscles with enough energy to keep up an extremely intense pace for very long, so you have to slow down. When you stop to rest, your body can regenerate the ATP you just used so you can perform another burst of energy.

- Anaerobic Energy System – When you perform a fairly intense activity for longer than about 10 seconds, your body has time to start utilizing the anaerobic energy system. The anaerobic system can produce energy very quickly and is able to maintain this production longer than the ATP-PC system. Most textbooks say the anaerobic system is capable of being the prime energy system for 2-3 minutes, but most people will not utilize the system that long before a rest is taken. The anaerobic system is typically used in conjunction with the ATP-PC and aerobic systems to produce energy. Soccer, rugby and basketball utilize this system to supply the energy needed for the extended periods of intense activity common to these sports. With training, significant improvements can be made in the efficiency of the anaerobic system in just 3-6 weeks. These improvements are usually very useful to sport performance because this type of training is quite specific (from an energy-system standpoint) to many sports.

- Aerobic Energy System – The aerobic system is the most efficient, but slowest, way to produce energy. This system will produce a nearly unlimited supply of energy, but it can't keep pace with the high demands of many sports that require a large amount of energy in a very short period of time. In most sports, the aerobic system will be used extensively, but never exclusively. It is the system that will help to replenish energy between plays when the body is nearly at rest and there is plenty of time before a burst of energy is needed.

Whenever the heart rate is elevated for an extended period of time, the aerobic system is contributing. A basketball game, for example, is full of short (under two minutes) periods of intense work, followed by periods of rest (time outs, fouls, etc.). During the play, the body is primarily utilizing the ATP-PC and anaerobic systems, but the aerobic system takes over as the primary energy producer during the rest periods while the heart rate is still elevated from the play. In fact, for many athletes, the heart rate can be elevated for the entire game, placing a large demand on aerobic metabolism.

Changes in the aerobic system are generally measured by the body's ability to utilize oxygen during a VO2 Max test. Changes in VO2 Max seem to take a much longer time than the other two systems, and genetics seem to play a large role in a person's ability to make significant improvements. It also appears that inducing a change requires extensive aerobic exercise, such as distance running, which is actually counterproductive for many sports because this type of training is so different than the sport.

Understanding the basics of these energy systems will help coaches understand how to create conditioning programs that are specific to the requirements of the sport. This also sheds some light on the misuse of aerobic conditioning in preparation for many sports.

Agility Drills for Conditioning

Using agility drills for conditioning is an excellent way to prepare for both the metabolic and neuromuscular demands of a sport. Straight-ahead running on a track will effectively train the metabolic pathways used in a sport, but the movement patterns are severely neglected in this type of "track" workout. Most athletes are required to perform numerous starts, stops, and CODs during competition, so using drills that closely mimic both the metabolic and movement demands of the sport will elicit the greatest positive transfer of training to sport performance.

Most experts agree that training the anaerobic energy system requires somewhere between a 1:2 and 1:5 work-to-rest ratio. A 1:2 work-to-rest ratio means that the rest interval should be 2 times the length of the work interval. So, if the drill lasts 10 seconds, the rest period between reps should be 20 seconds.

There is quite a difference between 1:2 and 1:5, so it's important to understand the differences. The shorter the rest period, the more metabolically challenging the training will be. This is good if metabolic conditioning is the only goal of training. The flip side of this low work-to-rest ratio is that the intensity and quality of movement will quickly decrease due to fatigue.

A higher work-to-rest ratio, such as 1:5, will allow the quality of movement and intensity to remain high during the workout. This is particularly beneficial when new movement patterns are being learned or for sports that allow for a relatively long rest between plays, such as football or baseball. This longer rest interval will not train the anaerobic or aerobic pathways as intensely as the shorter rest intervals. There is not a better or worse work-to-rest ratio, but the training goal must be clear when choosing rest intervals.

In team training situations, agility drills can be set up with specific work-to-rest ratios in mind. Let's say you have 15 athletes on a basketball team, and your goal is to train sport-specific movement patterns. You may choose one of the 3-cone drills listed in Chapter 6, and create a variation that resembles the movements you wish the athletes to train. Since your goal requires that the intensity be high with an emphasis on nervous system training, the rest intervals should be relatively long, for example 1:4.

To make this happen efficiently, you break the team up into three groups of five players and you set up the 3-cone drill for each group (so there are three, 3-cone drills laid out on the floor, one for each group). The first player in each line runs through the pattern twice, goes to the end of the line, and the next player steps forward for his/her turn. The coach gives the command, the next athlete takes his/her turn, and this pattern continues for as long as the coach wants. In this case, each athlete will rest while the other four athletes in the group run through the drill. As long as the athletes in each group are relatively close to the same speed, this creates a 1:4 work to rest ratio.

If the goal is to train the anaerobic energy system for sport-specific fitness and a 1:2 ratio is preferred, simply create five groups of three players. If there are "left-over" athletes (i.e. only 2 in one of the groups), instruct that group to leave an empty space between them so everyone performs the same amount of work. If the coach wants to keep the groups the same, but wants to give more rest between work intervals, simply pause for a period of time between athletes before giving the signal to go. This will lengthen the rest interval and allow the athletes more recovery time.

This is a simple concept that will help a coach set up drills and change the metabolic or neuromuscular emphasis of the training. The main idea is to give longer rest periods for movement pattern training and shorter rest periods for anaerobic conditioning. The work and rest periods do not have to be absolutely precise as long as this concept is understood.

Pure Speed vs. Functional Speed

Many coaches mistakenly put a tremendous emphasis on evaluating the pure speed of an athlete rather than his/her functional speed, or game speed. While pure speed is certainly a predictor of functional speed, the two are not synonymous.

Pure speed is defined as an athlete's ability to perform a straight-line sprint one time. Pure speed is demonstrated in a 40-, 60-, or 100-yard dash test, where the athlete only needs to perform the sprint one time, without any external variables to react to.

Functional speed is an athlete's ability to perform speed-dependent maneuvers throughout a competition. An athlete with good functional speed will be able to perform optimally at any time, even with external variables to react to, or at the end of the game when fatigue begins to affect performance. Many people call this "game speed" because there are many athletes who may not be able to perform an outstanding 40-yard dash time, but appear to be lightning quick on the field. Jerry Rice is an excellent example of an athlete with decent pure speed but amazing game speed. In fact, Rice was completely overlooked by many NFL teams because of a lackluster performance in the 40-yard dash at the combine. Yet, on the field he is one of the most explosive and successful receivers of all time.

Every year we hear about a college football player's NFL draft stock dropping because of an average 40-yard dash performance at the combine. Even though he may have dominated college football, his ability is immediately questioned because of his performance on a test that may never be duplicated on the playing field. And every coach has had an athlete who tests extremely well, yet appears to be slow on the field. Interestingly, a study on the NFL combines revealed a trend that the athletes who dominate the tests typically receive less playing time and have shorter careers than athletes who perform well (but not incredible) on the tests.

Functional speed also takes conditioning into consideration, involves the ability to accelerate, change directions, anticipate an opponent's movement and is clearly more important than pure speed for most sports. Unfortunately, many coaches and scouts still view pure speed as a vital part of the selection/recruitment process. Because this will not change any time soon, it is important to practice pure speed tests such as the 40-yard dash. Without decent pure speed numbers on paper, many coaches will not even take the time to look at an athlete's game speed.

Sample Training Programs

While a cookie-cutter approach is never the best way to design a program, it is sometimes helpful to have a basic plan to work from. These programs may be used exactly as presented, or you can amend them in a variety of ways. The key to successful program design is to make it appropriate for each situation. And, even if the drill is a good choice, never use a drill that you do not feel comfortable implementing. When first creating programs, it is advisable to write it down ahead of time, and you may even want to rehearse or practice to make sure there is enough time. With experience, you should be able to create programs very quickly (or even on the fly) depending on the situation that presents itself at the time of practice. Always be flexible, because situations change and you need to be able to adapt. For example, if an athlete comes to practice injured, modifications need to be made to create an effective training session.

Some drills, such as the Wheel Drill, lend themselves better to larger groups, while other drills, such as Angle Drills or Reaction Drills, are best used with individals or small groups. For optimal training results, vary the use of these sample workouts so that overall athleticism is developed.

Chapter 9 Coaching Tip

When designing long-term performance-enhancement programs, change the training emphasis from day to day for maximum development of overall athletic ability. For example, a soccer player training three days per week may emphasize linear speed one day, agility the next, and conditioning on the third day. Also take the strength-training program into consideration. The day after working the legs, for example, the athlete will be sore and unable to perform speed-and-agility drills optimally. Keep this in mind when planning workouts.

Team Workout for Learning Agility (Multi-Directional Sports)

Drill	Sets	Explanation
Warm-Up		
4-Square Drill	4-8	Use lines on the field or court. 10-20 sec/rep.
2-Line Teaching Drill	10-20	Focus on technique. Do multiple variations with long rest periods.
Short Sprints	4-10	Emphasize intensity.
Zig-Zags	3-6	Use varying the distances. Focus on technique.
Wheel	4-6	Vary the movement on each rep for sport-specificity.
Over 2, Back 1	2-4	Use varying movement patterns for sport-specificity.

Small-Group Workout (Multi-Direction Sports)

Drill	Reps	Explanation
Warm-Up		
Ladder Drills	Varies	Spend 5-10 minutes working on body control
Short Sprints	4-8	Focus on correct technique and intensity. Plenty of rest between reps.
Angle Drills	3-5 for each angle	Keep intensity high with long rest periods. Use at least three different angles.
Zing-Tao	4-6 each way	Focus on correct technique.
3-Cone Drills	4-6	Pick 2-3 sport-specific drills, and perform 4-6 reps of each.
JK Lane Drill	4-8	Focus on good movement transitions.
Mirror Drill	4-8	5-20 seconds per rep. Introduces reaction to opponent.

Individual Workout (Multi-Directional Sports)

Drill	Sets	Explanation
Warm-Up		
Squat-Jumps	2-4	6-10 reps/set. Can use additional resistance.
Bounding	2-6	Distance=20 yards. May incorporate lateral bounds.
Sprint Starts	6-10	Focus on technique.
Short Sprints	4-10	Focus on correct technique and intensity. Plenty of rest between reps.
Angle Drills	3-5 each angle	Keep intensity high with long rest periods.
Diamond Drill	4-8 each way	Focus on good movement transitions.
3-Cone Movement Changes	10-15	Focus on good movement transitions. Choose sport-specific movement patterns and vary the movements.
4-Cone Reaction Drill	5-10	Works on appropriate physical responses. 20 sec/rep.

40-Yard Dash Workout

Drill	Sets	Explanation
Warm-Up		
Bounding	2-4	Distance=20 yards
Frog Hops	2	Distance=20 yards
Box Jumps	3	10 jumps/set onto a 12-24" box. Add weight vest if technique is excellent.
4-Square Patterns	4-8	Use a variety of patterns, 1 & 2 legs.
Wall Pushes	2	20 seconds/set
Sprint Starts	6	Focus on technique with full recovery between reps.
Resisted Starts	4	Use a sled or or tubing. Full recovery between reps.
Starts	2	No resistance.
40-Yard Dash	2	All out effort on each rep.
40-Yard Dash	2	Use a weight vest
Backpedaling	4	Distance=20 yards. Use a sled, vest or tubing when technique is excellent.
50-Yard Dash	4	Only allow 30 seconds between reps. All-out effort on each rep.

100-/200-Meter Sprint Workout

Drill	Sets	Explanation
Warm-Up		
Bounding	2-4	Distance=20 yards
Frog Hops	2	Distance=20 yards
Tuck Jumps	2	20 reps/set. Pull knees high, jump quickly off ground.
Dot Drill Patterns	4-8	Use a variety of patterns, 1 & 2 legs.
Resisted 40-Yard Dash	2	Use a weight vest or sled. Full recovery between reps.
200-Meter Sprint	2	Use a weight vest. Full recovery between reps.
400-Meter Sprint	1	Use a weight vest. Full recovery between reps.
Backpedaling	4	Distance=20 yards. Full recovery between reps.
400-Meter Sprint	4	No resistance. 2 minutes rest between reps.
800-Meter Sprint	2	No resistance. 2 minutes rest between reps.
200-Meter Sprint	2	No resistance. 2 minutes rest between reps.

Anaerobic-Conditioning Emphasis Workout

Drill	Sets	Explanation
Warm-Up		
4-Square Patterns	6-10	Keep rest periods brief
Wheel Drill	4-6	1:1-1:2 Work:Rest, vary the movement patterns
Over 2, Back 1	4-6	1:3 Work:Rest, vary the movement patterns
Diamond Drill	4-6	1:3 Work:Rest, vary the movement patterns
Mirror Drill	4-6	1:2 Work:Rest, 10-30 seconds/set
Full Contact T-Drill	4-6	1:3-1:4 Work:Rest
300 Yard Shuttles	3	1:3 Work:Rest

Combine-Training Workout

Drill	Sets	Explanation
Warm-Up		
Squat-Jumps	2	6 reps/set
Weighted Squat-Jumps	2	6 reps/set
Vertical Jumps	2	6 reps/set, pause between each rep to work on technique
Resisted Sprint Starts	4-8	Use a weighted vest, sled, or tubing
Sprint Starts	4-8	No resistance, focus on technique
Pro Agility Shuttle	10-12	Practice both sides, focus on technique
40-Yard Dash	4-6	May add resistance for 2 of the sets
Incline Sprints	6-10	If available, perform short sprints on hill or treadmill
Position-Specific Drills	4-8	Each set will include 4-6 position-specific patterns.
Bench Press Workout		There are many bench press training programs available. Practicing the 225-lb bench press should be done as a part of a complete strength-training program.

Plyometric Workout

Drill	Sets	Explanation
Warm-Up		
Squat-Jumps	2	6 reps/set
Weighted Squat-Jumps	2	6 reps/set
Linear Bounding	2	10 reps/set, distance=20 yards
Lateral Bounding	4	10 reps/set, distance=20 yards. Hold the landings on the first two sets.
1-Footed Box Jumps	2	6" box, 10 reps/set
2-Footed Box Jumps	4	18-24" box, 10 reps/set
Skaters	4	20 reps/set
Lateral Box Hops	4	12" obstacle, 10 reps/set
Long Jumps	2	10 jumps/set. Hold landings on first set
4-Square Patterns	10	10 seconds/set. Change the pattern on each set.

Weekly Training Schedules

The following charts give examples of weekly training programs for different training goals or situations. While these routines may be optimal, scheduling conflicts will inevitably arise. Class schedules, competitions, mandatory days off, and practices may not fit neatly into these routines. Modify each routine accordingly so that each conflict is addressed.

Combine Training

Monday	Tuesday	Wednesday	Thursday	Friday	Saturday	Sunday
Starts	Upper Body	Plyos	Off	Agility	Plyos	Off
Sprints	Core	Lower Body		Patterns	Sprints	
Plyos				Core	Upper Body	
Patterns					Light Legs	

Off-Season Training

Monday	Tuesday	Wednesday	Thursday	Friday	Saturday	Sunday
Speed	Sport Skills	Plyos	Off	Speed	Off	Game **or**
Agility		Agility		Sport Skills		Light Skills **or**
Total Body		Upper Body		Total Body		Off

In-Season Conditioning

Monday	Tuesday	Wednesday	Thursday	Friday	Saturday	Sunday
Sport Practice	Sport Practice	Sport Practice	Sport Practice	Sport Practice	Sport Practice	Off
Total Body	Agility		Agility	Total Body	Conditioning	
	Conditioning					

Pre-Season Conditioning

Monday	Tuesday	Wednesday	Thursday	Friday	Saturday	Sunday
Conditioning	Agility	Easy Practice	Agility	Sport Practice	Off	Sport Practice
Sport Practice	Sport Practice		Conditioning	Conditioning		Conditioning
Upper Body	Lower Body		Upper Body	Lower Body		

Linear-Speed Emphasis

Monday	Tuesday	Wednesday	Thursday	Friday	Saturday	Sunday
Starts	Tech. Work	Plyos	Off	Starts	Plyos	Light Running
Sprints	Upper Body	Short Sprints		Sprints	Sprints	Tech. Work
Plyos	Core	Lower Body		Upper Body	Lower Body	
Conditioning				Conditioning	Core	

References

Anshel, M. & Novak, J. (1989) Effects of Different Intensities of Fatigue on Performing a Sport Skill Requiring Explosive Muscular Effort: A Test of the Specificity of Practice Principle. *Perceptual and Motor Skills* 69:1379-1389.

Baechle, T. & Earle, R. (2000) *Essentials of Strength Training and Conditioning,* 2nd Edition. Human Kinetics.

Baker, D. & Nance, S. (1999) The Relation Between Running Speed and Measures of Strength and Power in Professional Rugby League Players. *Journal of Strength & Conditioning Research* 13(3):230-235.

Belli, A., Kyrolainen, H., & Komi, P. (2002) Moment and Power of Lower Limb Joints in Running. *International Journal of Sports Medicine* 23(2):136-141.

Bobbert, M. (1990) Drop Jumping as a Training Method for Jumping Ability. *Sports Medicine* 9(1):7-22.

Bompa, T. (1994) *Theory and Methodology of Training,* 3rd Edition. Kendall/Hunt Publishing.

Brittenham, G. (1996) *Complete Conditioning for Basketball.* Human Kinetics.

Brzycki, M. (2000) *Maximize Your Training.* Masters Press.

Chu, D. (1992) *Jumping Into Plyometrics.* Leisure Press.

Cipriani, D., Abel, B., & Pirriwitz, D. (2003) A Comparison of Two Stretching Protocols on Hip Range of Motion: Implications for Total Daily Stretch Duration. *Journal of Strength and Conditioning Research* 17(2):274-278.

Cissik, J. (2004) Means and Methods of Speed Training, Part 1. *Strength & Conditioning Journal* 26(4):24-29.

Craig, B. (2004) What is the Scientific Basis of Speed and Agility? *Strength & Conditioning Journal* 26(3):13-14.

Davis, S, Barnette, B, Kiger, J, Mirasola, J. & Young, S. (2004) Physical Characteristics That Predict Functional Performance in Division I College Football Players. *Journal of Strength and Conditioning Research* 18(1):115-120.

DeCavitte, D. (2004) Personal communication.

Delecluse, C., Van Coppenolle, H., Willems, E., Van Leemputte, M., Diels, R., & Goris, M. (1995) Influence of High-Resistance and High-Velocity Training on Sprint Performance. _Medicine & Science in Sports & Exercise_ 27(8):1203-1209.

Dintiman, G. & Ward, B. (2003) _Sport Speed,_ 3rd Edition. Human Kinetics.

Frappier, J. (2004) Personal communication.

Hoffman, J., Cooper, J., Wendell, M. & Kang, J. (2004) Camparison of Olympic vs. Traditional Power Lifting Training Programs in Football Players. _Journal of Strength & Conditioning Research_ 18(1):129-135.

Karp, J. (2001) Muscle Fiber Types and Training. _Strength & Conditioning Journal_ 23(5):21-26.

Kawamori, N & Haff, G. (2004) The Optimal Training Load for the Development of Muscular Power. _Journal of Strength & Conditioning Research_ 18(3):675-684.

Komi, P.V. (1992) _Strength and Power in Sport._ Blackwell Scientific Publications.

Kukolj, M., Ropret, R., Ugarkovic, D., & Jaric, S. (1999) Anthropometric, strength, and power predictors of sprinting performance. _Journal of Sports Medicine & Physical Fitness_ 39(2):120-122.

Kyrolainen, H., Belli, A., & Komi, P. (2001) Biomechanical Factors Affecting Running Economy. _Medicine and Science in Sports and Exercise_ 33(8):1330-1337.

Kyrolainen, H., Komi, P., & Belli, A. (1999) Changes in Muscle Activity Patterns and Kinetics With Increasing Running Speed. _Journal of Strength & Conditioning Research_ 13(4):400-406.

Locki, R., Murphy, A. & Spinks, C. (2003) Effect of Resisted Sled Towing on Sprint Kinemetics in Field-Sport Athletes. _Journal of Strength and Conditioning Research_ 17(4):760-767.

Mannie, K. (2003) _Spartan Football Strength & Conditioning Manual._

Mayhew, J., Piper, F., Schwegler, T., & Ball, T. (1989) Contributions of Speed, Agility and Body Composition to Anaerobic Power Measurement in College Football Players. _Journal of Applied Sports Science Research_ 3(4):101-106.

McKenzie, D., Clement, D., & Taunton, J. (1985) Running Shoes, Orthotics, and Injuries. _Sports Medicine_ 2(5):334-347.

Meckel, Y., Atterbom, H., Grodjinovsky, A., Ben-Sira, D., & Rotstein, A. (1995) Phsiological Characteristics of Female 100 Metre Sprinters of Different Performance Levels. _Journal of Sports Medicine & Physical Fitness_ 35(3):169-175.

Mero, A., Komi, P. & Gregor, R. (1992) Biomechanics of Sprint Running: A Review. *Sports Medicine* 13(6):376-392.

Nesser, T., Latin, R., Berg, K., & Prentice, E. (1996) Physiological Determinants of 40-meter Sprint Performance in Young Male Athletes. *Journal of Strength & Conditioning Research* 10(4):263-267.

Nummela, A., Rusko, H., & Mero, A. (1994) EMG Activities and Ground Reaction Forces During Fatigued and Nonfatigued Sprinting. *Medicine & Science in Sports & Exercise* 26(5):605-609.

Phelps, S. (2001) Speed Training. *Strength & Conditioning Journal* 23(2):57-58.

Poleman, R., Walsh, D., Bloomfield, J, & Nesti, M. (2004) Effective Conditioning of Female Soccer Players. *Journal of Sport Sciences* 22(2):191-204.

Porcari, J., Pethan, S., Ward, K., Fater, D., & Terry, L. (1996) Effects of Training Strength Shoes on 40-Yard Dash Time, Jumping Ability, and Calf Girth. *Journal of Strength and Conditioning Research* 10(2):120-123.

Sale, D. (1988) Neural Adaptation to Resistance Training. *Medicine and Science in Sports and Exercise* 20(5 Supplement):S135-S145.

Sawyer, D., Ostarello, J., Suess, E., & Dempsey, M. (2002) Relationship Between Football Playing Ability and Selected Performance Measures. *Journal of Strength and Conditioning Research* 16(4):611-616.

Schmidt, R. (1991) *Motor Learning and Performance: From Principles to Practice.* Champaign, IL: Human Kinetics.

Swanson, S. (1998) Muscular Coordination During Incline Treadmill Running. *Masters Thesis.* University of Massachusetts - Amherst.

Swanson, S. & Caldwell, G. (2000) An Integrated Biomechanical Analysis of High Speed Incline and Level Treadmill Running. *Medicine & Science in Sports & Exercise* 32(6):1146-1155.

Wakeham, T. (2003) *Michigan State Volleyball Strength & Conditioning Manual.*

Wakeham, T. (2004) Personal communication.

Wenzel, R. & Perfetto, E. (1992) The Effect of Speed Versus Non-speed Training in Power Development. *Journal of Applied Sport Science Research* 6(2):82-87.

Weyand, P., Sternlight, D., Bellizzi, M. & Wright, S. (2000) Faster Top Running Speed are Achieved with Greater Ground Forces Not More Rapid Leg Movements. *Journal of Applied Physiology* 89(5):1991-1999.

Wilson, G., Newton, R., Murphy, A., & Humphries, B. (1993) The Optimal Training Load for the Development of Dynamic Athletic Performance. *Medicine & Science in Sports & Exercise* 25(11):1279-1286.

Yap, C., Brown, L., & Woodman, G. (2000) Development of Speed, Agility, and Quickness for the Female Soccer Athlete. *Strength & Conditioning Journal* 22(1):9-12.

Young, W., McDowell, M., & Scarlett, B. (2001) Specificity of Sprint and Agility Training Methods. *Journal of Strength & Conditioning Research* 15(3):315-319.

Young, W., McLean, B., Ardagna, J. (1995) Relationship Between Strength Qualities and Sprinting Performance. *Journal of Sports Medicine & Physical Fitness* 35(1):13-19.

Young, W., & Pryor, J. (2001) Resistance Training for Short Sprints and Maximum-speed Sprints. *Strength & Conditioning Journal* 23(2):7-13.

Index

About the Author

Jim Kielbaso is the director of the Total Peformance Training Center in Wixom, Michigan (www.totalsportscomplex.com). He holds a B.S. in Exercise Science from Michigan State University and a M.S. in Kinesiology from the University of Michigan. Jim is a Certified Strength & Conditioning Specialist (CSCS) with the National Strength & Conditioning Association, and a Certified Personal Fitness Trainer with the National Academy of Sports Medicine. He served as the Strength & Conditioning Coach at the University of Detroit Mercy from 1996-2002 and earned the distinction of Strength & Conditioning Professional of the Year for the Midwestern Collegiate Conference (now the Horizon League) in 1998. He was also an adjunct faculty member at UDM,  teaching several courses in the Department of Sports Medicine. Jim was the State Director for the National Strength & Conditioning Association from 1998-2004, and serves as a Regional Coordinator for the NSCA. He has produced a video on manual resistance strength training and has authored numerous articles as well as a chapter in the book *Maximize Your Training*. Jim has also been a featured presenter at clinics, camps, and conferences across the country. Having worked with thousands of athletes at all levels of competition (youth, high school, national level, collegiate, Olympic and professional), Jim has developed a unique movement-training program that can enhance the athleticism of any competitor. Jim lives in Plymouth, Michigan with his wife, Elaina, and two sons, Cameron and Drew.

To find out where Jim will be speaking, visit www.crewpress.com.